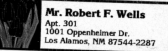
Suzhou

Shaping an Anc
for the New Ch
An EDAW/Pei W

D0478941

Text by Helaine Kaplan Prentice

S P A C E M A K E R   P R E S S

Washington, DC

Cambridge, MA

Front cover: Photograph by Mike Chen.
Other photographs by Mike Chen, pages 4, 6.
Additional photography by Jim Stickley
and Jeff Rapson of EDAW.

Publisher: James G. Trulove
Art Director: Sarah Vance
Designer: Elizabeth Reifeiss
Printer: Palace Press International

ISBN: 1-888931-15-9

Acknowledgments

I would like to extend an overarching thank you
to Peter Walker for recognizing the pressing need
for publications which document the art and
range of the landscape architecture profession,
and committing his own considerable energies
and the resources of his firm to addressing that
need. Thanks to those entrusted to carry out the
vision, the Spacemaker Press team: publisher Jim
Trulove, art director Sarah Vance and designer
Elizabeth Reifeiss. Their experience and sense of
style have helped make this volume a worthy addition to a body of work that is giving new sub-
stance to the literature of landscape architecture.

Those involved with the Suzhou Workshop
were forthcoming and still brimming with fresh
recollections months after the event. Many thanks
for interviews to: I.M. Pei and T'ing Pei; C.F. Tao
and Paul Tao; at EDAW, Joe Brown, Bob Pell, Jim
Stickley, Elizabeth Gourley and Jeff Rapson;
photographer Mike Chen; and from China,
Qiu Xiaoxiang, Wu Jiang and correspondents
He Xiaojun, Wang Ying, Wang Yi and Lin Yun.

On the frequent occasions when the writing
of this book gave me pleasure and satisfaction,
I dispatched a grateful thought to Doug Findlay
who introduced me to the fast-paced and fasci-
nating environment at Peter Walker and Partners,
where he is a partner.

For research assistance, I would like to
thank Carole Winckel, City of Portland, China
scholar Marjorie Fletcher, architect Hasan-Uddin
Khan, and the librarians at the Center for Chinese
Studies Library, University of California, Berkeley.

Finally, my husband, Blair Prentice, merits
praise beyond measure as colleague, compatriot,
and editor of first resort.

Helaine Kaplan Prentice
Berkeley, California
July 1998

Suzhou

**Shaping an Ancient City
for the New China:
An EDAW/Pei Workshop**

Contents

Prologue

This is the story of how, at a watershed in the history of China, an international team of planners was summoned to Suzhou to chart a sound course for the ancient canal city, a unique cultural resource whose heritage buildings and gardens are threatened by development pressure.

The plan that emerged was excellent, but of greater significance was the process that brought the plan about, a process that introduced to China a new way to sustain historic property, that granted permission to Chinese participants to envision the future, and empowered them to produce a bona fide plan. The 1996 Suzhou International Workshop Plan presents specific steps for the city of Suzhou to reclaim the Ping Jiang district and equip it with a new economic foundation.

China is seducing business and industry with its potential market of 1.2 billion consumers. The mood is forward-looking and hell-bent on development. The Communist Party has adopted a socialist market economy that according to *Forbes* magazine "looks more market and less socialist all the time" as the remedy for the poverty and outmoded conditions which have stymied the ambitions of this enormous country. Suzhou stands squarely in the path of the juggernaut.

Western design professionals in unprecedented numbers are taking on jobs in developing countries. Differences in language, culture, business ethics, and, in many cases, the residue of Communism, pose formidable barriers to effective consulting work abroad. The tale of the landscape architects and economic planners on the EDAW/Pei team and the workshop they conducted in Suzhou illustrates important lessons from one such assignment. This a story featuring smart and resourceful people, but in solving the problems, no single person stands out. The workshop is the hero.

Part One:

Seeking a New Approach

Recent development on the western
edge of Suzhou.

In November 1994, confronted by the swift
and often indiscriminate change overtaking old
Suzhou as streets were widened, picturesque
features razed, and new buildings imposed without regard to established local style, Mayor
Zhang traveled to New York City to seek advice
from illustrious architect I.M. Pei.

Development versus historic preservation is a familiar struggle, but as with most things in China, it is manifested in extreme, dramatic form. Suzhou, the imperiled resource examined here, is twenty-five hundred years old, a storied enclave of scholars and artisans, envied for its waterways and villas, and still possessed of the world's greatest collection of traditional Chinese gardens. The appetite for development is just as extreme; Suzhou[1] (pronounced SUE-JOE) is 50 miles west of voracious Shanghai, where "at any given moment fully one-fifth of the world's high lift cranes are at work" and construction is under way at twenty-five thousand sites.[2] Shanghai is vying with Hong Kong to become the business capital of China, and all Jiangsu Province—not least the city of Suzhou—wants a piece of the action. For economic vitality, the Yangtze River corridor[3] ranks a close second to the southeast provinces nationwide, even though it is a relative latecomer compared to Guangdong, the first commercial zone opened to Western business.

The trip from Shanghai to Suzhou, once a slow journey on the Grand Canal, is now about an hour's drive on an expressway still under construction. At freeway speed, tall passengers bump their heads on the roof of the car, while right alongside, in unpaved lanes, farmers, goats, and families with

babies in carts, proceed on foot, the entire scene a metaphor for the coexistence of rapid development and rural ways in China.

Westerners envision an anonymous central authority in Beijing that regulates the particulars of daily life in China. But at the local level, political power is vested in a system of familiar faces, a municipal mayor and district deputies who take an ardent interest in the welfare of their town. Although the mayor is not elected by popular vote, the trappings of a kind of democracy are to be found in this Chinese version of Chicago's ward system or New York's district planning boards, which divvy up decision-making in American cities.

In fact, many an American city would be fortunate to have a leader like Suzhou's Zhang Xinsheng, a cosmopolitan man who became mayor in 1989. *Time* magazine listed Mayor Zhang on the "*Time* Global 100," a roster of rising stars worldwide. *Fortune* magazine labeled Zhang "brainy but unpretentious," and credited him with Suzhou's triumphs in economic development. Fluent in English, Zhang learned business and management in the United States; he is an avid student of Western culture, a devotee of Mark Twain, blues and jazz, and, unusual for a Chinese national, enamored of cheese. Mayor Vera Katz of Portland, Oregon,

Suzhou's sister city, said, "One of the many things about Mayor Zhang that has impressed me most is his enormous curiosity and understanding of what is happening in the world."

In November 1994, confronted by the swift and often indiscriminate change overtaking old Suzhou as streets were widened, picturesque features razed, and new buildings imposed without regard to established local style, Mayor Zhang traveled to New York City to seek advice from the illustrious architect I.M. Pei. Since the Ming Dynasty, Suzhou has been the Pei family's ancestral city, and it was I.M. Pei's grandfather who stemmed an earlier invasion—in a literal sense—by fending off rapacious warlords with diplomacy and cash inducements. As a child, I.M. Pei played in Stone Lion Grove (Shizi Lin), the classical garden the family owned in Suzhou, and in 1992, he and his wife, Eileen, celebrated their fiftieth wedding anniversary there.

"Mayor Zhang presented himself well to my father," recalls urban planner and developer T'ing Pei, who attended the initial meeting at the elegant Madison Avenue architectural offices. But I.M. Pei, at age 77 still much sought after as a charismatic leader in matters of design, was by necessity selective about the projects he took on. He was cautious about encouraging the mayor. Pei was not inter-

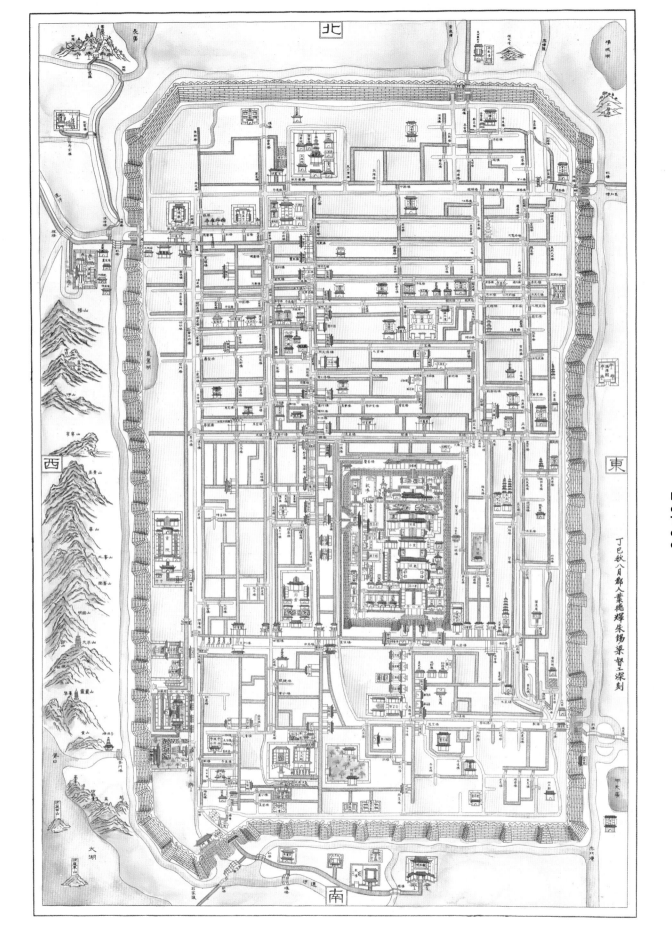

北

西

東

南

丁巳秋八月郡人葉德輝朱錫梁暨工深刻

Map of Suzhou, from a stone
engraving dated 1229 A.D.
The study area, Ping Jiang
district, is in the northeast
quadrant.

9

Pei observed . . . what he thought the first two steps should be: clean the water in the canals, then plant willow trees to beautify them. Where the canals become moat, the willows would also mark the boundary of the vanished city wall.

ested in wasting time on decorative notions that lack driving force. Without agreeing to do anything, Pei applied his prestige in a manner that launched a plan for Suzhou that would have real value.

"Look," declared I.M. Pei from behind his circular black spectacles, "I need to know there is real commitment to do something." Will the provincial government and the central government get behind this? Will they dedicate the personnel, the funding, to see this plan through? "Because," he persisted, "the problems of this city transcend the city itself. And the cost of taking meaningful steps is beyond the resources of Suzhou."

Pei observed to his son what he thought the first two steps should be: clean the water in the canals, then plant willow trees to beautify them. Where the canals become moat, the willows would also mark the boundary of the vanished city wall.

Just as in the twelfth century, Suzhou is surrounded by a medieval moat, and for eight hundred years had been enclosed by a mighty wall that defined as much as defended the inner city. The wall was 10 meters thick, with six gates—one on the north, one on the south, and two each on the west and east walls.[4] During the Cultural Revolution (1966–70), the Red Guard demolished large sections of the Suzhou city wall, and along with it

the boundary and sense of place that such a potent structure provides. The land long occupied by the wall was usurped by factories and squatters. Abruptly, the character changed. The rudest uses should be routed out, Pei recommended to his son T'ing, and if the wall cannot be rebuilt, then define the edge by planting trees. A fast growing waterside tree, like the graceful willow, seemed to fill the bill.

"I guess that I thought that tree planting was rather a casual approach to it," offered the deferential younger Pei. T'ing Pei's frequent visits to China and his many projects in Asia made him better acquainted than his father with the dilemmas facing modern Suzhou. "Even cleaning up the canals wasn't going to do anything. It's a first step, but it's only a symbolic step, and it doesn't really protect and preserve the old city."

Meanwhile, Mayor Zhang must have had a successful year on the home front making his case for Suzhou, for in November 1995 a distinguished delegation appeared in New York: Yang Xiaotang, vice governor of Jiangsu Province, and the secretary of the Communist Party in Suzhou, Xu Shudong. Their presence signified political support for the preservation of Suzhou as a cultural asset, and for costly improvements to roadways and utility systems—the

Willow-lined canal in the Ping Jiang.

"For me the starting point was, 'Is there really an economic future for this?'" explained T'ing Pei. "Because you can't make it a museum. You can't make a whole big city a museum."

infrastructure of a modern city. The vice governor carried with him a message from a vice premier in Beijing which presumably stated, but in any case signified, support at the central government level. The entourage satisfied I.M. Pei's prerequisite regarding water quality in the canals—the government would devote resources to begin the necessary water treatment and diversion work—and with that, T'ing Pei was tapped to represent his renowned father and see the effort through.

For a second time, while appearing to step aside, I.M. Pei endowed the nascent Suzhou plan with the means for realization, for in the person of his hand-picked delegate, his Harvard-educated elder son, was a no-nonsense urban planner who recognized the primacy of sound economics in any vision for development, or, for that matter, any vision for preservation.

"For me the starting point was, 'Is there really an economic future for this?'" explained T'ing Pei. "Because you can't make it a museum. You can't make a whole big city a museum."

A thoughtful man with an endearing chuckle, descended perhaps from his father's habitual smile, T'ing Pei sized up the situation in old Suzhou. First, the building stock is extremely old, in disrepair, and has no obvious economic purpose. It is occupied by piecework factories and residences with-

out any services. Furthermore, the sector is low density, two stories high—even with a lot of crowding, it's still low density by urban standards—and significantly lacking in any infrastructure. People still draw water from wells right next to polluted canals. "I mean, what's this water like?" Pei mused. "They use chamber pots, and they just go swish that stuff out into the canals." (Others, more discreetly, set their "honey pots" outside the door for collection at dawn by a woman with a primitive red cart. The accumulated contents are disposed of out of sight, though many suspect in the very same canals.) The cost of installing modern utilities in a low-density area like this is by any measure—per foot, per square meter, per capita, or per shop—prohibitively expensive.

T'ing Pei elucidated the problem further. With the exception of the heritage gardens and Ming dynasty houses, one building is not more intrinsically valuable than another. Nor would you even want to save individual buildings—it's their collective character that is significant: the buildings that, alone, are not important become tremendously important taken together. And finally, the old city must compete with unencumbered new towns and suburbs to attract investment, especially lucrative foreign investment.

In China, longstanding relationships with a patina of trust and accountability are central to business affairs. Western "networking" seems superficial by comparison. Notwithstanding Mayor Zhang's credentials and drive, it was his pivotal connection with Hong Kong developer C.F. Tao that secured his entrée to I.M. Pei and set this project in motion. I.M. Pei's good friend C.F. Tao has been developing real estate in China for twenty years with his brother S.P. Tao, ever since foreign capital was introduced in 1978. The Jinling Hotel in Nanjing, developed by the Tao brothers, was among the first examples. The Jinling Hotel is a wholehearted monument to Western technology and glamour so compelling that locals are drawn to the gleaming tower as a dramatic setting for family snapshots in the same way that tourists might pose in front of the pagoda on Suzhou's Tiger Hill.

In the early 1980s, the Jiangsu provincial government appointed Zhang Xinsheng assistant general manager of the Tao brothers' Jinling Hotel. At thirty-six stories, it was the tallest building in China at the time, and no foreign operator dared run the hostelry because of the paucity of tourists. To manage this highly visible symbol of Western style was a heavy burden. Under Zhang's direction the Jinling Hotel broke even the first year, and soon turned a profit.

With the exception of the heritage gardens and Ming dynasty houses, one building is not more intrinsically valuable than another. Nor would you even want to save individual buildings—it's their collective character that is significant: the buildings that, alone, are not important become tremendously important taken together.

"It was Joe who proposed the workshop approach." . . . The workshop format demands that effective drawings and documentation be produced by a rigid deadline and immediately presented in a public forum to an influential audience. Reams of sketches are involved, as is on-site study and nonstop discourse, in a stimulating, if somewhat frenetic, atmosphere.

14

In 1996, it was developer C.F. Tao, recognizing a worthwhile cause in competent hands, who sponsored the study of old Suzhou sought by Zhang, by then Suzhou's mayor for seven years.

"Even before I agreed to do this," recalled T'ing Pei, "I knew that I didn't have the means to tackle this kind of job on my own." So he went to someone he had known for twenty-five years, someone with the right credentials. He went to Joe Brown, president and CEO of the international planning firm EDAW, headquartered in San Francisco, with a substantial practice in Asia. "It was Joe who proposed the workshop approach," related Pei. "I thought it was brilliant."

The idea jelled during Pei and Brown's exploratory visit to Suzhou in March 1996, when they assessed how much useful work the available fees could support. The weather was dreary, raining all the time, and chilly. The pair of trenchcoat-clad Americans held their black umbrellas aloft. "We were outside slogging around, but I think Joe was quite taken with the whole thing," Pei said.

Joe Brown is energetic—a warrior of world travel on behalf of the firm—and entertainingly talkative. His satisfaction from the Suzhou Workshop telegraphs in every reference to the method and the result.

Brown arrived in Suzhou with a workshop in mind: two weeks of long days, fertile collaboration, and occasional confrontation, to solve a complex planning problem as rigorously as possible given the time constraint. This approach, also known as a charrette, assembles students or local citizens to frame the solution collectively under the guidance of professional urban designers. The workshop format demands that effective drawings and documentation be produced by a rigid deadline and immediately presented in a public forum to an influential audience. Reams of sketches are involved, as is on-site study and nonstop discourse, in a stimulating, if somewhat frenetic, atmosphere.

EDAW has conducted intensive design workshops for two decades in the United States with landscape architecture and planning students who are selected competitively by application to act as an arm of the firm. The Suzhou workshop departed from the familiar pattern when Yan Daoming, director of the Suzhou Urban Construction Bureau and cosponsor of the enterprise, stipulated that half the traditional "student" positions be assigned to his best junior professionals. The rest could be filled by young Chinese men and women enrolled at national architecture schools.

Part Two:

The Workshop Begins

Moated city and modern environs

On a muggy day in the middle of July 1996, eight design professionals descended from distant points upon Suzhou, China: four landscape architects, three city planners, and an engineer; three hailed from San Francisco, two from Hong Kong, and one each from New York, London, and Denver. The San Francisco contingent toted twenty rolls of yellow trace, four dozen markers, pushpins, pencils, triangles, and templates; base maps at three different scales; slide carousels, a small library of books, custom tee-shirts and hats imprinted with the workshop logo, and so on down to Post-it® Notes, kneaded erasers, and drafting dots, all loaded into three duffels and three suitcases which they had crammed into a taxicab the day before on the other side of the date line in California.

Marco Polo himself visited the city of Suzhou in 1276 and found everyone from clerk to courtesan clothed in silk. Suzhou is famous still for silk production, with two silk factories in the study area, though one must venture well south of town to encounter a mulberry tree. The EDAW/Pei entourage has traveled here to bring ideas from the West and, like the intrepid Venetian who became confidant and advisor to the Kublai Khan, to exert some influence.

Marco Polo dubbed Suzhou "a great and noble city," and the team had come to protect the greatness and nobility expressed in physical form over the centuries. China looks to the United States for development expertise; the Chinese want to learn from our achievements. But they need to learn from our mistakes, to recognize the toll exacted on American city centers by misguided urban renewal in the 1960s. The ancestral heart of Suzhou, a city cherished by all Chinese, deserves a better fate. The study area, a district called Ping Jiang, meaning "river on the flat land," is located in the northeast quadrant of the old city and comprises 40 hectares.[5] The new arrivals quietly hoped that their work in Ping Jiang would set the standard for preservation and development throughout Suzhou.

On Sunday, July 14, the 1996 EDAW/Pei Workshop convened at the government-owned Jian Wei Hotel in Suzhou. There were fourteen Chinese workshop participants—six studying architecture at a university or institute, eight employed by the Suzhou Planning Bureau.[6] To have been selected is an honor, and honorific distinctions have great currency in China. When the students were asked why they signed on, Ye Jing, department of architecture, Southeast University, extended the most poetic reply: "She is so similar to me, the ancient gardens, the canal, the people and so on, that I am eager to contribute myself to make her more beautiful."

The Jian Wei Hotel is a utilitarian structure located at Number Eight Zhongguo Lao Lane, a 15-minute walk from Ping Jiang. The group of 24 would reside there, eat there, and work day and night in a large conference room which had just been redecorated as a gesture of hospitality. It was freshly painted high-gloss white, and paint fumes infused the air-conditioned chill. Rows of chairs faced one narrow table in the front, like soldiers in formation. The hotel had been asked to construct some layout tables, and these were lined up along the walls.

"The first thing we did was to tear all that apart," recalled project manager James Stickley from EDAW's San Francisco office. "We made five big, equal work tables, and moved them right to the center of the room. That was the first cultural change. Workshops are about teams and teamwork, and no one's up at a head table lecturing down to you. You're all involved equally."

This upset the hotel manager no end. The unruly Americans, in dispensing with his orderly arrangement, had erased all trace of hierarchy.

Furniture notwithstanding, the introductory sessions consisted of formal papers presented by local experts on planning subjects that set some Chinese students to dozing; they did not ask any questions, nor did they interact. It was the first sign

Marco Polo dubbed Suzhou "a great and noble city," and the team had come to protect the greatness and nobility expressed in physical form over the centuries. . . . The new arrivals quietly hoped that their work in Ping Jiang would set the standard for preservation and development throughout Suzhou.

Field work began in the main marketplace, Ping Jiang Lane, which occupies six or seven blocks along a canal on the east edge of the site, and bursts into activity twice a day when vendors sell their wares.

of an endemic passivity that, if indulged, would disable the workshop process. The Westerners endured translated presentations, impatient for the hands-on to begin. "The only thing that's going to save us is the schedule," thought Joe Brown at the time, "because we're not going to let these papers be delivered past day two."

Site Visit

Site visits are always a welcome relief from the confining aspects of a charrette. Field work began in the main marketplace, Ping Jiang Lane, which occupies six or seven blocks along a canal on the east edge of the site, and bursts into activity twice a day when vendors sell their wares. In this district there are no supermarkets; a typical sight is the delivery by moped of a doze n live ducks hanging by their feet in six-packs from the ends of a bamboo pole. Any detritus, of course, is tossed into the water. Stickley knew that keeping the market on Ping Jiang Lane would be essential to the plan. "The market serves a social function far larger than the exchange of goods for money. But we have to rethink the disposal of corn husks and fish guts."

On Cang Street, several grain warehouses survive from the era of the wondrous Grand Canal.

Declared the longest artificial waterway in the world, the 1,500-mile-long Grand Canal is a north-south artery linking four east-west running rivers, and thereby uniting all China since the seventh century.[7] The Grand Canal brought grain from the fertile fields in the south to feed the hungry north, and over time bestowed on its river cities, like Suzhou on the Yangtze, a lively prosperity born of trade.

Most of the population of 350,000 in old Suzhou inhabit aging residential structures at densities unimaginable when they were built as courtyard villas for a single family.[8] The vernacular architecture is a handsome ensemble of simple forms, rough and smooth, dark and light. White plaster walls meet clay roof tiles glazed the blue-black of a still pond at twilight. On long, narrow lots, the houses face inward, perimeter rooms framing a series of protected courtyards. The ubiquity of the style contributes much to the identity and appeal of old Suzhou, though the inhabitants would quickly abandon these archaic buildings for indoor plumbing and central heat.

With crowding, the spaces, once eminently civilized, realign, and boundaries dissolve. You can't tell one house from another. Where before a wall defined territory, now a set of behaviors presides.

An embedded door frame is discovered in an alley wall.

On long, narrow lots, the houses face inward, perimeter rooms framing a series of protected courtyards. The ubiquity of the style contributes much to the identity and appeal of old Suzhou, though the inhabitants would quickly abandon these archaic buildings for indoor plumbing and central heat.

To penetrate a housing block, instinct leads you down an alley. It seems a public passageway at first, but transforms unannounced into a private hall, and you find yourself, abashed, looking straight into a tiny kitchen with a family of five, and something boiling on the stove. Not wanting to intrude, you beeline for what seems to be a common space, a simple, stone courtyard, but it turns out to be a private extension of living quarters. Three elderly women and an old man jump up from their wooden stools. Another corridor is dark as a tunnel, the footing dirt and, for all you know, pitted with holes. Unexpectedly, the passageway releases you into an open court, an actual public space, and you find yourself squinting from the unaccustomed light even though it is a dim, rainy day. How could such a cavern be the path to a common yard?

The participants native to Suzhou escorted the others, and knocked on courtyard doors. "Walking through that courtyard door, we entered another world," recounted EDAW's Elizabeth Gourley. "We were experiencing their lives."

Robert Pell, EDAW economist from the London office, had another take on the dissolution of boundaries. "We walk around the site, and Mr. Qiu, the planning director, says 'You'll be interested in this house,' and he opens the door and walks in.

We just walk through people's houses, through their kitchens, through their sleeping areas, and he waves at things and says, 'This is interesting. Look at the water pouring in through the roof.' Then we turn around and go out. There is no privacy. Can you imagine walking into somebody's apartment in the projects of southeast London with the chief planner and a group of Chinese delegates? You wouldn't get out alive."

By the end of a day's touring—maps soggy, shoes wet—everyone was ready to kick back with a Dong Wu beer, the local brew,[9] ponder the experience of Ping Jiang, and devise the evening's amusement. But this is what separates the landscape architect on duty from the tourist; at the end of the tour, the professional's work has just begun. The site visit is a commencement—a wellspring of facts, problems, and inspiration—not an objective in and of itself; in this case, however, the impression of having been a tourist was central to the job at hand.

Exploring a courtyard in Ping Jiang
Left to right: **Jim Stickley, Joe Brown, Qiu Xiaoxiang (in doorway), Paul Tao.**

The gardens are reason enough to stay for several days. Only in Suzhou can the visitor experience an unrivaled collection of Chinese classical gardens.

After Beijing and Shanghai, Suzhou is among the top four tourist cities in China, and the number one tourist destination in Jiangsu Province. In 1995, Suzhou recorded nearly eight million Chinese-visitor days and 350,000 foreign-visitor days. Average spending per day: Chinese, 450 RMB; foreign, 1,200 RMB. There are currently three thousand hotel rooms in the city, forty-five hundred in the metropolitan area. The Suzhou Tourism Bureau estimates a need for two thousand more hotel rooms in the next three years. The EDAW/Pei plan proposes 112,000 square meters of tourist accommodation in Ping Jiang, 104,000 of which are new construction, and 27,000 square meters of accessory retail and restaurants.

The Potential for Tourism

Suzhou is a natural tourist attraction, underused. The challenge for Suzhou is to create multi-day visitation, and urged by T'ing Pei, that challenge drove the workshop plan. "Let's put it this way," he said, abbreviating the theory of multiplier effect, "You've got to get people to drop money in the city." They have to spend at least one night, more is better: they stay in a hotel, eat at a restaurant, do some shopping, visit a museum, then take in more sights the following day. That's how to create jobs and capture the economic benefit. A healthy tourist environment lures business visitors as well. "If people just go in and out and buy a few trinkets from a souvenir stand, it doesn't do a helluva lot for the local economy," he observed.

The gardens are reason enough to stay for several days. Only in Suzhou can the visitor experience an unrivaled collection of Chinese classical gardens. Chinese classicism, like Western classicism, refers to an age-old esthetic code central to the visual identity of the culture. Like any such code, it consists of recognizable elements that can be recombined in countless ways, and with the application of artistry achieve the sublime. The oldest well-preserved example, Surging Wave Pavilion Garden, dates from

the middle of the Northern Song Dynasty (960–1126 A.D.). The Stone Lion Grove, owned for a time by I.M. Pei's family, was built in the late Yuan Dynasty (1206–1368). Seven more gardens survive from the Ming Dynasty (1368–1644), the Humble Administrator's Garden being the largest and best known. Other gardens that are open for viewing were begun or reconstructed after the reign of Emperor Tong Zhi (1862–1874), and uphold the canon of Chinese landscape design.

The Chinese garden is beautiful and serene, the essence of Chinese art. Painting, calligraphy, poetry, and garden design evolved together; garden design brought the metaphorical qualities they shared to life. In the confines of an urban garden, remote, untrammeled nature as depicted in paintings—the mystical isles of the immortals, the wild mountains and ravines, the streams and placid lakes—was made manifest by hillocks, pools, rock piles, and plants of symbolic importance. The garden was a statement: here dwells a person of refined sensibility who wishes to live in seclusion on a distant mountainside contemplating nature, but for now must make do with Suzhou's benevolent domain.

The idea of a mountainside vantage point was important. In Chinese painting, the viewpoint floats above the ground plane, as if the painter were an

Couple's Retreat Garden

24

enlightened, weightless being. "This dream of immortality seems to inform all Chinese art, as though art itself were a middle distance between the visible and the invisible," wrote Geoffrey and Susan Jellicoe in *The Landscape of Man*. Within the gardens are raised pavilions that seem poised in mid-air with their upturned eaves. The pavilions were sited to capture discreet views of nature distilled, as if taken in from a thatched-roof cottage on said mountainside. Amidst a stillness that fostered contemplation, the owner would take tea and pen verse. Today, such contemplation is hard to come by with the tourists filing through, as they do in so many of the great gardens of the world, including the Japanese gardens and eighteenth-century English gardens better known in the West, though indebted to the classical Chinese antecedents found in Suzhou.

It is rare for landscape architects to find themselves in a place where their profession has been esteemed for centuries. For a thousand years, Suzhou attracted scholars, aristocrats, and high-ranking officials who chose the city expressly to own a garden there. Chinese garden designers were often artists who could depict their inner vision, but the gardens were constructed by craftsmen who held the wild hills in their souls. "Experts in piling-up rockery were never those who could write

poetry or paint pictures," wrote seventeenth-century poet Li Yu. "Yet when one saw them casually lifting a rock and placing it upside down, it instantly became gray and forceful as in calligraphy or tortuous and graceful as in a painting."[10]

The very names of Suzhou's gardens and pavilions are enchanting. Some, like the Humble Administrator's Garden and the Retired Fisherman's Garden, refer to their patrons (in their new guise as rustic sage); some suggest desired mood: Happy Garden, Carefree Garden, Lingering Here Garden, and the Hall of Thirty-Six Lovebirds; others, like the Pavilion of Snow Fragrance and Luxuriant Cloud, are meant to induce a celestial state; still others describe the aspect of nature they are meant to portray: the Mountain Villa of Embracing Emerald, the Pavilion of Pine Wind Heard, and the Tower of Juxtaposed Views.

Heritage tourism is a two-way street. In order to catch a traveler's eye, Suzhou must protect and restore its historic resources. Beside the gardens, these include specific landmark buildings and, more pertinent to the workshop, the fabric of the city, that is, the patterns woven by commonplace old structures huddled on narrow lanes and overlooking canals that give Suzhou its charm. Not all of

The problem is that the Chinese do little in the gulf between high rise and restoration. The concept of preservation development, and its many gradations, long accepted in Europe and now a centerpiece of revitalization efforts in many American cities, is unknown in China.

Ancient water gate at southwest corner of perimeter moat.

old Suzhou is as intact as Ping Jiang; there have been modern intrusions and a rush to widen streets for the automobile. In return, preservation creates a powerful identity that attracts growth on the strength of image alone.

An oft-cited reference during the two weeks, and the yardstick favored by sponsor C.F. Tao, was the Clarke Quay project in Singapore, which transformed a historic warehouse district on the Singapore River into a bustling retail center by playing off the historic architecture. Clarke Quay, built in 1993 and based on an EDAW site plan, is evidence that success breeds success. The stores, restaurants, and boat slips became commercially viable quickly enough to help pay for higher quality renovation.

The considerable amount of construction taking place in China today falls at two ends of the spectrum. At one extreme lies the scholarly (though infrequent) reconstruction of ancient cultural sites; at the other, where most building activity is concentrated, the development of brand new high rises on greenfield sites. Witness the crop of apartment towers erupting like corn from the fertile bottomlands of the Yangtze Delta region.

A preeminent example of new development is the China-Singapore Suzhou Industrial Park, a 28-square-mile enclave on the city's east side, and the largest of Singapore's investments abroad. Manufacturing sites are abetted by office buildings, apartment blocks, and shopping areas to create a planned environment attractive to multinational companies. Samsung makes semiconductors here, Advanced Micro-Devices makes circuit boards, Nabisco bakes Ritz Crackers, and Eli Lilly produces Prozac.

A different epoch in commerce is conjured up by the Drama Museum, a typical preservation project. In China long ago, remote towns and provinces founded men's clubs in major cities where business travelers from their precincts could meet and stay. The Drama Museum was such a lodging, outfitted with stage and orchestra pit for entertainment. It is located in the study area and has been restored.

The problem is that the Chinese do little in the gulf between high rise and restoration. The concept of preservation development, and its many gradations, long accepted in Europe and now a centerpiece of revitalization efforts in many American cities, is unknown in China.

Developer and workshop sponsor C.F. Tao is an innovator in this regard. He has produced for modern executives a version of the genteel surroundings enjoyed by the learned aristocracy in Ming Dynasty Suzhou as part of his new development west of the old city, Suzhou Garden Villas. The canalside architecture is a crisp, geometric rendition of time-honored forms—central courtyards, gray roof tiles, circular gateways in white plaster walls—with the added luxury of space and light.

Tao advised Brown to teach the Chinese how to fuse historical sites with new markets and devise development schemes. "It's teaching," Tao counseled, "but it's teaching with a point of view."

The Workshop Divides

Elizabeth Gourley and He Xiaojun.

To protect the historic core, the plan proposes fourteen singular landmarks, like Wang House and Pan House, once the courtyard homes of wealthy merchants, for restoration as cultural attractions.

The workshop students were divided into five concentration teams to tackle the components of the plan that would rev up the tourism engine, namely: Historic Preservation, Redevelopment Sites, Market Potential, Open Space and Circulation, and Water Quality and Infrastructure. Each team was headed by an EDAW professional who pitched right in.

"That saved us," allowed Joe Brown. "In the States we take a freer approach, 'Well, what do you all think?' Every time the students try to get direction, we turn it back to them. We're constantly giving leadership away." But the Chinese students were not accustomed to asserting themselves.

Suzhou Planning Director Qiu Xiaoxiang recognized the predicament: "People in U.S. say everything could happen. In China we say, it's too hard, we can't do that, no change." Westerners are open to possibility, while the Chinese are constrained by what exists, explained the 33-year-old bureau chief.

Despite that, it was difficult during the first week to keep the students focused on their team assignment because everyone kept trying to solve the whole thing. "It's hard to accept being in a subgroup when you're full of big ideas," empathized Jim Stickley. The Western planners were there to assist a society moving away from collectivization,

and now they had to coax the students back together to come up with a collaborative scheme. Every two days the five teams would gather to compare notes and discuss strategy.

Historic Preservation

Landscape architect Elizabeth Gourley, head of the historic preservation group, had ventured to China twice before. She speaks some Mandarin, has a degree in anthropology, and was at ease in the Chinese culture. "Elizabeth was very effective in Suzhou," assessed Brown, "and all the women students were drawn to her. She drew beautifully, she thought beautifully, and they all wanted that." Lizzy, as the women called her, might have seemed exotic to them—she is tall, blond and accomplished—yet her gentle manner has an Eastern sensibility, so the women might have sensed something familiar, too.

Wang Ying and He Xiaojun, two women graduate students on Gourley's team, were passionate about improving services in Ping Jiang for the people who lived there. They perceived the plan from the inside, and if it strayed too far toward commercial tourist development, they resisted. Wang Ying and He Xiaojun made certain there were places for child care, for example, and facilities for the elderly. They

intended to keep the social aspects of the neighborhood intact along with the architecture.

The team took inspiration from Xu Minsu, deputy director of the Tourism Bureau and author of the definitive book on the vernacular architecture of Suzhou. As they became absorbed in the details of Xu Minsu's illustrations and their own on-site sketches to devise a typology, they almost lost track of the bigger picture and the need to move on to a plan.

Gourley noticed how sparing the students were with the yellow tracing paper, reusing small or wrinkled pieces she would have thrown away. This, and an attempt to operate the Suzhou Planning Bureau's hoary copy machine, were sobering reminders that beyond the well-equipped conference room, and behind the ambitious, capitalist facade, was a third-world country with scarce resources.

Based on an earlier survey by the planning bureau that rated the architectural and historic quality of every structure in Ping Jiang, the team defined a large preservation zone in the center of the district, and on the western edge of the site along the historic market street at Ping Jiang Canal. To protect the historic core, the plan proposes fourteen singular landmarks, like Wang House and Pan House, once the courtyard homes of wealthy merchants, for restoration as cultural attractions. Other

Above: Student sketches illustrate the precious character of old Suzhou. *Below:* Proposed public space at historic well site.

Planning Director Qiu Xiaoxiang (pen in hand) and the historic preservation team. *Left to right:* Wang Ying, He Xiaojun, Tan Yin, Elizabeth Gourley, Yao Helin.

Temples are among the heritage properties tagged for restoration, but it is difficult to find them in Ping Jiang without an escort, concealed as they are behind unmarked courtyard walls.

significant buildings or complexes are to be renovated for housing or shops while preserving the architecture. Structures that detract from the district are to be replaced altogether with compatible infill designs. Two well-marked interpretive routes will wind through the historic zone, one outdoors, the other protected from the elements and thus including shopping areas and restaurants.

Temples are among the heritage properties tagged for restoration, but it is difficult to find them in Ping Jiang without an escort, concealed as they are behind unmarked courtyard walls. Some, like Wei Dao Taoist Temple, partially survive. Others were commandeered for industrial use during the Cultural Revolution, when communal work was tantamount to religion. The team visited a measuring-tape factory that had been a shrine to Confucius.

One current trend in China that bedevils old and new buildings alike is an infatuation with white tile and reflective blue glass. To stymie this and other impositions of taste that would compromise historic integrity in Ping Jiang, the plan prescribes ten ways to protect the architectural patterns that define Suzhou. Roof lines, for example, may vary according to building type as long as they adhere to precedent in the district, and, of course, the roofing material must bear the signature blue-black

glaze. The traditional Suzhou tiles are still manufactured; the building industry has not changed in China as rapidly as in the United States, so availability, or the higher cost of hand-worked products, is not the impediment to accuracy that it is here. Another guideline addresses gates: the opening cannot exceed two door widths, about two meters, and overhangs shall be adorned with the self-same tiles. A third restrains the building height along streets and alleys to one and two stories, maintaining sunlight and a human scale, while permitting greater height and density on the interior of the blocks. A fourth requires that the trim on windows and doors be painted dark colors. These are practical directives which do not increase building costs and can be achieved.

The air-conditioner, in particular, has altered the appearance of old Suzhou: the blessed but ungainly boxes protrude from white plaster surfaces and contradict the district's historic identity. Condensation from the units rusts the mounting racks, staining the walls below. Throughout southern China, walls are thus discolored; it looks unattractive and shabby. The plan proposes a disguise: in future renovations, air-conditioners should be recessed into the wall, the opening covered by ceramic lattice, and the condensate collected in a drain. Units that remain on the

outside should be concealed with a tiled shed roof, on the vernacular model for second-story porches.[11]

"Most of the old city's residents are low incomers, and they live in this district for too many years," wrote He Xiaojun in a letter dated February 24, 1997, from the School of Architecture, Tsinghua University, Beijing, her grammar and spelling unchanged here. "So I think the most important things for us is to protect the context, not only the architectural style but the people who live there. As far as the historic preservation, if our design benefit the people, not the rich man, we're success. This is the most important thing."

Redevelopment Sites

Jim Stickley, a sturdy veteran of seven design campaigns in Asia, was charged with detailing the Redevelopment Sites portion of the Suzhou plan. On his team were the two other women students in the workshop. Ye Jing, an undergraduate at Southeast University in Nanjing, was tiny and quiet, though when she spoke with her pen, Stickley said, she could really assert her ideas. Zhang Qin, an architect on the Suzhou Construction Committee, did not like Americans presuming to come in to teach the Chinese. One day at

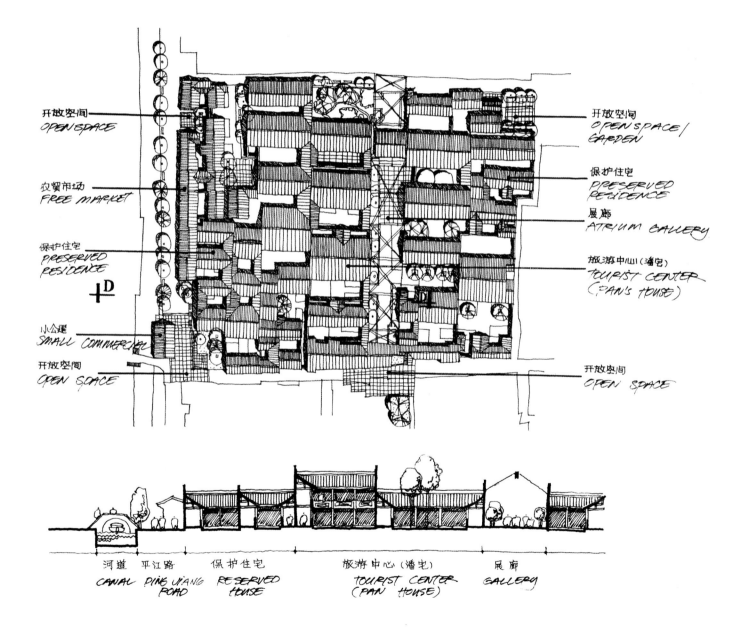

开放空间
OPEN SPACE

农贸市场
FREE MARKET

保护住宅
PRESERVED
RESIDENCE

小公建
SMALL COMMERCIAL

开放空间
OPEN SPACE

+D

开放空间
OPEN SPACE/
GARDEN

保护住宅
PRESERVED
RESIDENCE

展廊
ATRIUM GALLERY

旅游中心(潘宅)
TOURIST CENTER
(PAN'S HOUSE)

开放空间
OPEN SPACE

河道 平江路　保护住宅　　　旅游中心(潘宅)　　　展廊
CANAL PING JIANG RESERVED TOURIST CENTER GALLERY
ROAD HOUSE (PAN HOUSE)

Plan and section propose adaptive re-use of historic Pan House and upgraded housing to preserve the neighborhood near Ping Jiang canal.

That the "right" idea—in this case, a framework to preserve traditional patterns and design vocabulary—had been proposed by a local participant. . . .rather than the imported consultant, is the best possible turn of events in a charrette situation.

Left to right: Zhang Qin, Tan Donglin, Jim Stickley.

lunch she challenged Elizabeth, saying "You do not like the Chinese people in your country." Gourley shrugged this off as a stock statement, noting simply, "Zhang Qin was very strong, and she did not trust us."

But it was Zhang Qin who came up with the organizing concept for the residential redevelopment sites. She drew a sketch that for the first time in the workshop illustrated clearly how new construction would fit into the historic district, and her idea became the prototype for the plan. That the "right" idea—in this case, a framework to preserve traditional patterns and design vocabulary—had been proposed by a local participant, and an opinionated one at that, rather than the imported consultant, is the best possible turn of events in a charrette situation.

Workshop members in government employ were at times more resistant to the "transfer of technology"—that is, learning Western ways—than those still in school. In Stickley's group was a mid-level planner who often spoke in a piercing, high-pitched voice; he was soon dubbed "the Arguer."

The redevelopment team proceeded to identify parcels amenable to the desired tourist activities. Foremost, they needed hotel sites, but did not want to disrupt residential areas, nor could they intrude on the sacred historic core delineated by Gourley's team. The best location was the southeast part of Ping Jiang, where two undistinguished silk factories (one for weaving, one for dying) and a prison were logical candidates for removal. Confined to this corner, the tourists' comings and goings would not disturb tranquility in the residential quarter.

Relocating the prison off-site meant extra meetings with the mayor, the city, and prison officials, in whose analysis the cost of moving the prison included the cost of building a new one elsewhere. This was debated until, at last, the grim neighbor departed from the plan. In the new China, priming the flow of foreign investment can budge otherwise immovable obstacles.

Eliminating the factories and prison freed up enough real estate to create a critical mass of tourist accommodation: three brand new hotels—four-star, three-star, and business suites—a conference center, and a performing arts complex. Add to that a five-star inn adjoining the provocatively named Couple's Retreat Garden, ample commercial support in both new and adapted buildings, and remote parking, and the redevelopment plan introduces 145,000 square meters in direct support of tourism, excluding, of course, the canals.

Market Potential

It fell to EDAW economist Bob Pell and his squad to determine if there was enough redevelopment to attract the coveted investment, and to demonstrate that the numbers worked. "I admired China fifteen years ago," Pell told his colleagues, "and I was in a very small minority." He had majored in Chinese politics in the early 1970s at Southampton University in England,[12] but that was toward the end of the Cultural Revolution when travel to China was next to impossible, and so, despite his interest, he had never been. Since the fall of Communism in Eastern Europe, he has consulted on economic development in East Germany and Romania. Pell is by his own reckoning "numerate, but lousy at languages," which explains why he switched to economics when confounded by the study of Mandarin Chinese.

What intrigued Pell was the prospect of economic change. How do you take one economic function, the factories, out of the city center and replace that industry with another activity—probably Western-funded—that would become an engine of regrowth?

"I went out there full of hope, only to find it's incredibly difficult to get any data, to get beneath the first layer of generality. We must have heard

Suggested infill projects for silk factory sites.
Above: **Grand plaza,** *Below:* **Four-star hotel with interior garden.**

Ye Jing on the redevelopment team.

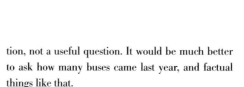

Bob Pell with members of the economic group.

"We had to start looking at it piece by piece. If you were a private investor, could you come here and make something work? We took each of the components and tried to find comparable examples."

the same, somewhat stilted, glossing-over of redevelopment essentials nearly every day."

A month before the workshop, Bob Pell and Jim Stickley went to Suzhou for a week to collect accurate figures on construction costs, government subsidies and loans, the value of land, any standing financial commitment to public works, and typical returns from sale, lease, or other business arrangements. Pell requested appointments with department heads in all the pertinent fields. He was expecting to meet them individually, as he'd done in East Germany, and to do so methodically over the first three days. But it soon became apparent that the interviews were not going to be arranged in the desired way at all.

"On about the fourth day," he continued, "they did set up one meeting, and everybody came. All the departments that we had wanted. At once. 'Well,' I said, to break the ice, 'could we go around the room and have everybody tell me what your vision is for this site in the future?'"

"That's not a good question," cautioned the translator. "A better question would be to ask them about what they do."

When Zhou Renyan, the governor of Ping Jiang district, arrived, Pell tried to elicit his vision for the area. Again he was reproached: this was a bad ques-

tion, not a useful question. It would be much better to ask how many buses came last year, and factual things like that.

"And so we asked," Pell continued, "'How long will it take to clean up the water?' and they replied, 'Three years.' Then we asked about the time involved to restore the historic houses and they replied, 'Three years.' And then we said, 'You know, we're worried about the prison here. You'll need to find a site for a new prison, build it, move all the prisoners, demolish the old prison. How long do you think that would take?'"

"Three years."

At this point Stickley leaned over to Pell and whispered, "What's all this about?"

"I think," said he, "we're two years into a five-year plan. If that person sitting in front of us says it'll take seven years, it implies that he knows what the next five-year plan is, and they don't. They're not allowed to."

Pell elaborated later, "We were going into an area that would take five, ten, fifteen years to develop. It would take that long anywhere in the world. But the participants are in a conceptual mindset of five-year plans."

"Three or four days into the workshop, we still had precious little data," Pell recalled, "and

people were asking, 'Where are the numbers? How are the numbers going to work?' I threw away my pro forma—I wasn't going to get any more data that I could use in it—and developed an appraisal model.

"We had to start looking at it piece by piece. If you were a private investor, could you come here and make something work? We took each of the components and tried to find comparable examples." The authorities in Suzhou had built some housing, call it Block 12. They had demolished just about everything except one vintage Ming house, and built anew. There were construction costs, and there were sales values—the government maintained that the houses were selling well—and the figures were current.

Then Pell's team got a reading from developer C.F. Tao on his sales values and construction costs at Suzhou Garden Villas, about three miles away. Tao's clientele is the expatriate market, the managers of multinational companies in the Suzhou Industrial Park who desire Western comfort. Apartments were selling for a quarter-million U.S. dollars, and villas for $450,000. From that the team could extrapolate: would something similar, but located next to a vibrant commercial and cultural center,[13] near the canalside park, as envisioned in the plan, attract expatriates to live in the middle of town? "I didn't feel that in two weeks we were expected to do a

**Vision for a pedestrian commercial street
along an existing canal.**

Left to right: Wan Chengxin, Ye Jing, Zhuang Yu, He Xiaojun, Wang Ying.

Parcel by parcel, they made their way through, using air photos and traipsing in the rain: how many hectares, how many families, how many stories tall?

market survey," replied Pell, but based on the numbers "we could safely say that if this site were made available, then probably in the next five years a developer would come in and sign on."

As for the beautiful Ming house on Block 12, it had reputedly been sold for a million U.S. dollars, to be restored as an artist's studio, sales room, and home; would others want to come to Suzhou and do the same? "Well, yes," Pell answered his own question, "quite possibly." The team was coming up with positive land values which could contribute toward the renovation of old buildings.

Then they had to pin down elusive values for the commercial components: shopping, entertainment, restaurants, and, especially, hotels. The Sheraton under construction on the edge of the old city seemed a promising source, but the appraisal that was provided turned out to use numbers as a self-fulfilling prophecy. Pell's students went round to existing hotels and got rack rates and estimates of the occupancy through the year. Factoring in the presumed cost of the land,[14] the Sheraton appraisal wouldn't add up. A substitute analysis was offered by the Construction Bureau, handwritten in exquisite Chinese characters. The team concluded that there is demand for good hotel sites in Suzhou, but they could not determine

if the release price could also support off-site improvements, like infrastructure, in Ping Jiang. Only the government could determine that.

Pell was stoking a spreadsheet on his laptop with all the data he could get first hand. Off his students would charge on their bicycles to have another look about, and to make sure the land budget was accurate. Parcel by parcel, they made their way through, using air photos and traipsing in the rain: how many hectares, how many families, how many stories tall? Pell fed the figures to his engineers to generate costs. "They're not big-picture crude estimates," Pell said, satisfied. "The numbers are actually built up from a hundred-parcel analysis. I was quite surprised we were able to get to that level of detail. It was good."

There is, however, one category of cost intrinsic to development in China that does not appear in the spreadsheet, and is euphemistically called "fees." "What sort of fees are they?" Pell inquired disingenuously. "Are they for building permits?" No, he was informed, they are just government fees, negotiable government fees. Unspecified fees are widely viewed as a major impediment to foreign development in China.[15] In the Suzhou Workshop Plan, a note in the text states matter-of-factly that all numbers shown exclude any government fees.

One student, Qi Gang, was keen to learn how to set up the models, and used the laptop whenever Pell left the room, even at lunch. Another student, however, was very rigid in his thinking. "No, this is the way it is" was his disputatious line.

Open Space and Circulation

Jeff Rapson, a production man from EDAW's Denver office with charrette experience and a Taiwan project on his résumé, headed the Open Space team. "It was a bunch of guys working," Rapson said to describe the understanding in the group that transcended language. More than that, it was something of a graphics brotherhood, its members drawn to what Rapson called "this incredible visual thing," the bridges and canals, the lanes and alleys, paths of travel at human scale and the remarkable long views they frame. Wang Yi, a graduate student in architecture at Tongji University in Shanghai, and architect Lin Yun, of the Suzhou Industrial Park Design Institute, sketched well in three dimensions, and when they set down confident renditions in blue ink on yellow trace, other teams soon enlisted their aid.

"I am driven," confessed Jeff Rapson, "product-oriented, and I knew how much product we had to generate." The students did not appear to compre-

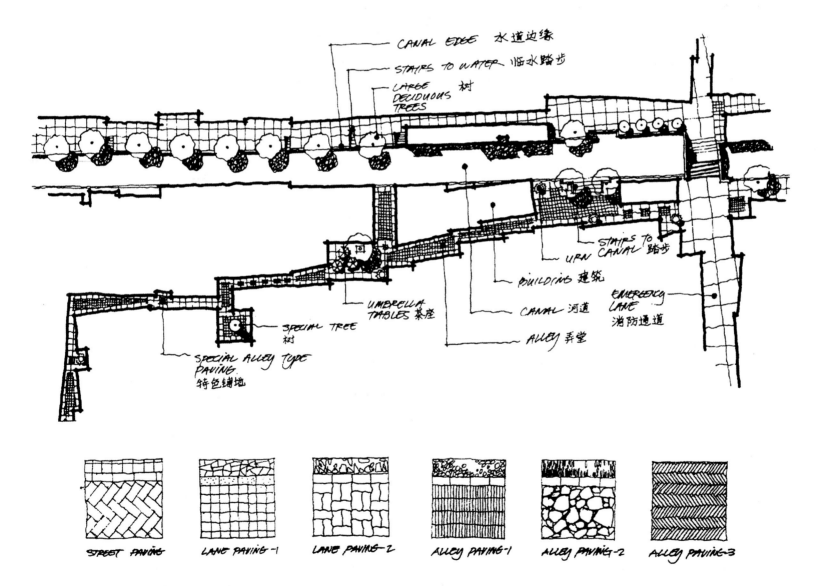

CANAL EDGE 水道边缘
STAIRS TO WATER 临水踏步
LARGE DECIDUOUS TREES 树
STAIRS TO CANAL 踏步
URN
BUILDING 建筑
EMERGENCY LANE 消防通道
CANAL 河道
UMBRELLA TABLES 茶座
ALLEY 弄堂
SPECIAL TREE 树
SPECIAL ALLEY TYPE PAVING 特色铺地

STREET PAVING   LANE PAVING-1   LANE PAVING-2   ALLEY PAVING-1   ALLEY PAVING-2   ALLEY PAVING-3

Paving design to enhance new construction is compatible with age-old motifs.

Jeff Rapson and the open space team.

Bridges are the delight of Suzhou, and abundant in variety: arched or flat, stepped or smooth, ornate or simple, protected or wide open to the sky.

hend the magnitude of the job. "They would take two hours off from noon to two—a daily rest period called *xiuxi*—to sleep or smoke or play cards. We'd have the mayor coming at four o'clock and all this work to do, so I ran around the hotel corridors banging on the doors, 'C'mon! C'mon!'" The Open Space team wrote funny little notes to Rapson in return. "You are a slave driver. We are very tired. You are working us too hard."

The plan makes the most of the existing open space network, augmenting it to handle new growth and tourism, and recognizing its dual role as circulation. The southernmost canal in Ping Jiang will become the main promenade in the study area; a pedestrian path is added to its unused side. "You really needed a stronger way to cross the site," Rapson explained, "so we came into that little canal and made it double-sided." The Da Xin Qiao canal forms the cross-bar in an "H," uniting Ping Jiang canal on the west edge of the district where the street market convenes, and another large canal on the east. Two abandoned canals are to be reinstated, one on the south side of Zhong Zhang Jia Lane because of its visible location on the southern edge of the district, the other parallel to the City moat, on the other side of the proposed new park.

Bridges are the delight of Suzhou, and abundant in variety: arched or flat, stepped or smooth, ornate or simple, protected or wide open to the sky. The plan adds to the tally and assortment, wisely suggesting modern versions as well as traditional ones in wood, concrete, and stone.

Water taxis would penetrate Ping Jiang on a proposed canal circuit that includes the lakes of East Park. When water quality outside the district permits, the circuit would be linked to the citywide network of canals. In the meantime, there would be a Ping Jiang stop for the city moat water taxi, connecting this district to the Suzhou train station and the old city at large.

Visitors who arrive by land in Ping Jiang would disembark from bus or car at a plaza[16] or in front of their hotel, and advance into the district on foot. Vehicles turn directly into a parking yard. A similar parking area is provided for future residents in the northerly part of the site, and a loop road handles emergency access, minimizing the need to widen quaint streets, a dilemma which had been thought insurmountable.[17] Most residents get around on bicycles, which can negotiate the alleys but inflict a surprising parking load.

The north-south axis is the time-honored organizing principle of Chinese cities and Chinese houses; the workshop plan accedes to this convention by making north-south Cang Street the new commercial spine, lined with shops, cafes, restaurants and tea houses. Another north-south corridor to be reinforced is the market at Ping Jiang Canal: vendors will be relocated from the street into storefronts to reduce debris in the water and ease circulation along Ping Jiang Road.

Ping Jiang district is very dense, with little by way of street trees or greenery. In its northeast corner, where merging canals widen to form a large pond, East Park offers respite from the confines of the maze. In a gesture benefiting residents and visitors alike, the plan proposes a linear extension southward from East Park the entire length of the canal. This park would be decidedly contemporary, the subject of a national design competition—a notion novel to China—or a site for a sculpture by I.M. Pei.[18] And what became of I.M. Pei's fancy to line the canals with willows? Apparently, the subject never came up.

Whereas American students these days are fueled by espresso drinks, the Chinese consumed cigarettes and bottled water. Smoke was especially a problem whenever the air-conditioning shut down as it took down the ventilation system with it. "There were a million cups all over the tables," recalled Rapson. At one frantic moment, alarmed by spills on the final drawings, he stood up and pleaded, "Can we keep all the water in the back!"

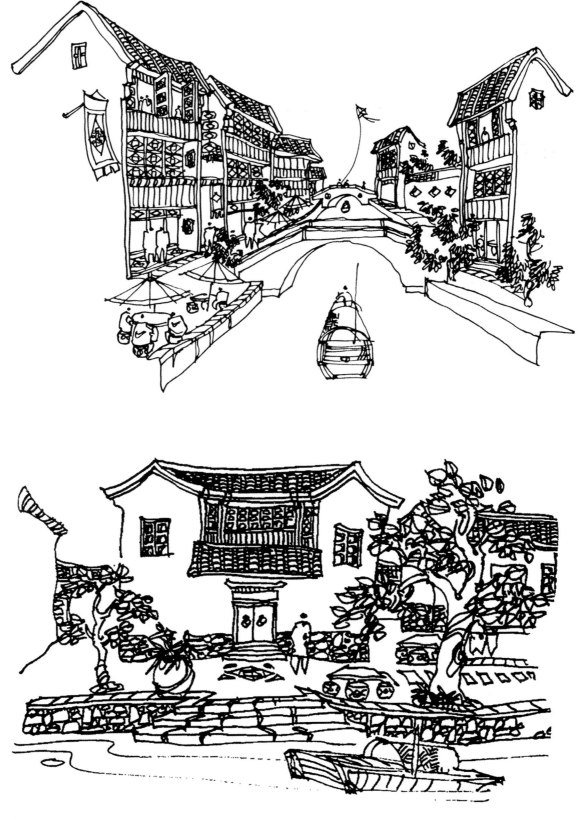

Sketches show revitalized canals. *Above:* **View of water-front hotels and cafes.** *Below:* **New water-taxi landing.**

Examining other canal cities for inspiration.

A substantial improvement to water quality in the moat and the canals is critical to the health of Suzhou residents, and the absolute prerequisite of tourism's bounty.

Water Quality and Infrastructure

A substantial improvement to water quality in the moat and the canals is critical to the health of Suzhou residents, and the absolute prerequisite of tourism's bounty. Environmental Planner Patrick Lau, director of EDAW/earthasia in Hong Kong, led the workshop team that tackled these gritty issues.

At present the water quality falls below the standard, which is unfit for human contact; poor sanitation practices are in part to blame, but also at fault are outmoded engineering and design. The storm water and foul water drainage are combined and discharged into the canals. The rate of flow in the canal is woefully slow because flood gates separate the canal from the moat, and the route of moat water from inflow port to outflow is interrupted by dead ends. Upgrading water quality to Grade III, suitable for boating, requires separate drainage for storm water and foul (said to be 30 percent complete in 1996) and a wastewater treatment plant (operational in 1997). Lau's team proposed diluting the water in the moat and moving it along with the cooling water from Wang Ting Power Plant; better moat water makes better canal water. Once replenished, the water level must still permit navigation; the cross-section of the canal must account for the draft of the boat, the foundations of adjacent buildings, the impact of the propeller on the canal bed, and clearance under historic bridges.

Workshop participants would harbor the memory of another water-related issue long after summer was gone. The still waters of Suzhou breed mosquitoes that bite with a vengeance, according to the victims, leaving marks that last for months. Mosquito abatement is not directly addressed in the plan, though improved water flow should help to alleviate the problem.

A complete renewal of utility service is suggested, with placement of all cable underground. At present, electricity, telephone, and television are brought in via overhead lines that are unsightly and in some cases worn dangerously thin. A high-voltage line crosses directly over populous quarters. There is no gas supply, nor are there fire hydrants; street lighting is found at the corners of alleys only. Ducted liquefied petroleum gas is recommended for each household, a sprinkler system for all historic buildings, and wall-mounted lights to illuminate public ways.

An innovation of the plan is the way eight utility lines are layered vertically underground in shared trenches in order to protect the scale of the street.[19] "At first, the Suzhou engineers didn't understand why we were making such a big deal of it," said Jim Stickley. "To them, wider is modern and modern is better." The workshop also challenges China's national standards for the distance of gas or water mains from adjacent buildings (3 meters), and for fire separation at end walls (6 meters), as these clearances are unrealistic in Ping Jiang.

Above: **Existing cross-section at Da Xin Qiao canal.**
Below: **Proposed improvements for access and water quality.**

Selling dried beans and spices alongside Ping Jiang canal.

And How Was the Food?

No story on China would be complete without a word about food, and indeed at Suzhou the eating arrangements impinged on the group dynamic. Typically, all members of a workshop dine together, regardless of stature; the meal is a chance to establish personal connections that promote the exchange of professional ideas around the drawing boards later on. In Suzhou, the mingling did not occur. Daily meals—described as "Chinese cooking the caliber of dorm food"— were taken in the hotel dining room; the students sat at tables separate from their foreign advisors. When a visitor came, like C.F. Tao or the minister of construction, the Westerners were whisked off to a special dining room for a ten-course meal, while the students consumed the same fare every night. "We were the honored guests, and the students were not. I found that rather odd," said Bob Pell.

"One night there was a banquet in another hotel," he continued with some embarrassment, "and I thought it was for the whole workshop. We came down and got into cars and were taken there and looked around and there were no students." The seating at the banquet was as rigidly prescribed as the behavior: the number-one man, Yang Xiaotang, vice-governor of Jiangsu Province, was positioned at the center of a long table, T'ing Pei on one arm, C.F. Tao on the other. Facing Yang sat Mayor Zhang, Brown and Pell at his sides. All the other people who were senior members of the project team were at the ends somewhere, and they did not speak the entire time. Only the six dignitaries were entitled to converse, which they did one by one through a translator. Everyone else spent two hours eating in silence.

"You just sit there with a big smile on your face while the turtle rolls by your plate," laughed Jeff Rapson. The turtle was huge, a foot and half in diameter, maybe two. It was wheeled out on a serving cart by two young women who spun the delicacy around on a lazy-susan for everyone's review. Then they removed the display to a side table and hoisted the turtle onto a chopping block. Within minutes the women returned proffering tiny porcelain bowls with a chunk of turtle shell in fishy broth. Pig's head on a platter was another privilege reserved for honored guests.

Fresh crayfish at Ping Jiang market.

Taking shelter from the rain in a pavilion at Lake Tai.

Meanwhile, others are caught in the storm.

Turning Points

Mayor Zhang called for a progress report at the end of the first week. The request got the adrenaline flowing and forced the students to surrender the passive role of protégés and affirm their ideas up on boards. "We had to get our headlines right, and get our diagrams on the wall, no matter how unpolished," recounted Brown, who gingerly managed to be part of the group but also the leader. "When the students saw what they had accomplished, and earned a reaction from the mayor, they couldn't believe it."

The weekend between sessions was devoted to touring the region; one contingent went southwest to explore the resort at Lake Tai, and for fun set out in two small rowboats. Liz Gourley was reluctant at first. To judge from the blackening sky, a thunderstorm was approaching, and the boats had metal frames overhead for canvas canopies. But the adventuresome students egged their teacher on, and in a role-reversal of leadership and trust, off they all went into choppy waters, their fates briefly joined. The wind picked up, the rain came down, and figures on shore started waving wildly for the adventurers to return. "I was afraid we would be swept away into China's largest lake and never return to shore," Gourley recalled with a rush. "By the time we got back, it was really pouring. We huddled under umbrellas, shuttling back to shelter two-by-two." A new bond had been formed.

The major ideas having coalesced by the end of week one, week two consisted of refining the concepts,[20] and of gearing up for the final presentation to important officials. At this point, the differences in background and expectation between leaders and students were brought into sharp relief.

The pedagogical model common in Asia casts the student as the recipient of the gift of knowledge; workshops like this one ask the student to be an active partner in learning. Chinese planners are said to ponder questions for a long time, a scholarly method that can become overwrought. The workshop, by contrast, is iterative by nature, a rapid evolution of thought and proposal that moves like a spark from one version to the next. And, of course, the workshop must come to an end, the deliberations shaped into presentable form; while it seems impossible to imagine architecture school or employment without production demands, many of the young professionals seemed unaccustomed to working against a deadline.

Also in the second week, fatigue set in, and some people drifted off after lunch. Even on the Friday of the final presentation, the students took their *xiuxi* to watch the Olympics televised from Atlanta. "We had to get a little bit tough, but in the end, they all respected that," Stickley said.

On Wednesday, the exhibits started taking shape and spirits revived. "We had been very clear in our own minds what this presentation was going to look like," Stickley said of the EDAW/Pei team, "but the Chinese students could not picture the final product until it started coming together. Then they all grew very excited, and there was a lot of forgiveness."

What really seemed to galvanize the teams and motivate each student to do his or her best was the momentum of collaboration and firm direction from above. Brown described it as "an aggressive, confrontational process in a passive environment about planning and design. You have to provoke, you have to interact" to stimulate the exchange of ideas. The Chinese participants, overcoming a cultural reticence to speak their minds, needed emphatic assurance that this was expected of them. In a letter, student He Xiaojun expressed the importance of a strong workshop leader, "I think Mr. Joe Brown is so powerful man," she wrote. "He put us to advance. I think this is the key of the success."

Stone pier, Lake Tai.

"You have to provoke, you have to interact" to stimulate the exchange of ideas. The Chinese participants, overcoming a cultural reticence to speak their minds, needed emphatic assurance that this was expected of them.

On charrette for the final presentation.

46

"For the Chinese, it was a good introduction to a more scientific methodology and systematic analysis of urban planning and design. . . . For the Americans . . . it brought a better understanding of the actual characteristics of Chinese culture in the old cities and how their Chinese counterparts think through those issues."

The Final Presentation

Amid the hustle to completion, C.F. Tao approached a harried Brown. "Now, Joe," he said, "let me just talk to the students for a few minutes in Chinese," and he took them aside and worked some magic. Perhaps it was the charm of the exalted sponsor, perhaps it was having a Chinese person take up the leadership reins, or the comfort of being addressed in their own language. They had seen Tao many times before; he dropped in every day to enjoy the pace and the mix of players. "EDAW best in the world!" was his upbeat refrain. But today, Tao addressed the students privately, and they warmed to his ministration.

At two o'clock that afternoon the conference room filled with distinguished guests, including Zhang Xinsheng, mayor of Suzhou, Zhou Renyan, governor of Ping Jiang, Yan Daoming, Director of the Suzhou Urban Construction Bureau, publisher James Trulove from Washington, D.C., developer Paul Tao, C.F. Tao's son, from Hong Kong, and photographer Mike Chen, from California. Adding to the buzz, a television crew had been dispatched to film this singular event, though not for the benefit of Ping Jiang residents (few of whom have access to television), but to inform the entire city and China's audience-at-large that good things, progressive things, were happening in Suzhou.

T'ing Pei officiated, but soon the floor was handed over to the students, for whom public speaking was an unfamiliar prestige. "Point your feet toward the audience," Brown had sensibly advised. "Don't hide in the drawing. But don't stay removed from it either. Touch the drawing as you talk. Everything will work out."

And it did. The 1996 EDAW/Pei International Workshop plan presented that afternoon creates a new economic purpose for the historic quarter of Ping Jiang. With multiple-night tourism as its premise, the plan has solid grounding: the ascent of global travel and the unlocking of China's gates combine well with the qualities of Suzhou as a tourist destination and, by association, as a nexus for business and industry. The city of Suzhou has already attained recognition and political clout for successful development on the outskirts of the old city; the workshop complete, the city is now poised to showcase the opportunity for investment in its singular urban core.

The proposal for Ping Jiang sets forth a mix of uses, a synergy between new and old. Historic integrity is Suzhou's greatest asset. The students used their lively sketches to ratify the inherent value of the old quarter. Residential blocks and market

A local reporter interviews
Qiu Xiaoxiang and Joe Brown.

Mayor Zhang Xinsheng.

streets are retained in the plan in established locations, with a prevailing north-south axis in the Chinese manner. The famous network of canals remains the unifying framework, and its role for transportation is improved. Byways in the heart of Ping Jiang remain narrow; classical gardens, landmark structures, vernacular architecture, and the happy assortment of bridges are respected and preserved.

Improvements were proposed to make the historic surroundings more livable. The Open Space and Circulation team illustrated how three loop roads in the plan accommodate automobiles, and canalside parks are expanded to accord more open space for recreation, footpaths, and bicycle travel. The Infrastructure team explained how fire-fighting access, utility service, street lighting and trash collection are to be provided, in some cases for the first time. Water quality in the canals is substantially upgraded with construction of a storm-water drainage system and an off-site wastewater treatment plant. A generous volume of fresh water will accelerate canal flow.

As the presentation unfolded, new buildings were proposed on sites chosen by the Redevelopment team, including five hotels concentrated in the southeast quadrant of the district, making the most of this highly visible location in the moated city. Three of the hotels displace activity conducive neither to tourism nor to a residential neighborhood (factories and a prison). New commercial uses spawned by the hotels, like restaurants, shops, and services, occupy nearby buildings. Infill construction is guided by the Historic Preservation team's design directives aimed at perpetuating the characteristic elements of old Suzhou.

The students unfurled a carefully drawn concept plan for Ping Jiang that synthesized the recommendations of all five teams. The plan is distinguished by a holistic approach that melds ideas from different disciplines, interweaving solutions to separate problems to advance a common goal.

Grand plans in developing countries often suffer from poor strategies for implementation. The Suzhou workshop plan avoids this problem by recommending a master developer, an approach tested elsewhere in southeast Asia at different scales, including entire new towns. The master developer is responsible for a multitude of things: guarding the plan's original vision, marketing key sites, initiating direct development, soliciting investors, constructing the public improvements, insuring consistent quality between separate elements of the scheme, and creating confidence that the entire plan will come to fruition.

The plan recommends that the role of master developer for Ping Jiang be played by a joint venture of the government and the private sector. Only then would cross-subsidy from the most profitable elements of the plan to those that require support be assured. For precedent, the students pointed to the successful partnership, albeit between two governments, at the familiar China-Singapore Suzhou Industrial Park.

On an overhead projector, the Market Potential team demonstrated with charts and figures that the plan could generate positive land values and therefore attract foreign capital, given government sponsorship of public works that benefit the district as a whole. C.F. Tao had urged the students to make a solid case so the city could approach the central government and say, "Here is the exact amount of money it will take to leverage private investment in Suzhou."

Tao praised both the immediate and the long-term benefits of the workshop. "For the Chinese, it was a good introduction to a more scientific methodology and systematic analysis of urban planning and design. It helped to broaden their thinking and open up their imagination. For the Americans, I think it brought a better understanding of the actual characteristics of Chinese culture in the old

The sojourn in China ratified the EDAW philosophy that a Western approach cannot be imposed wholesale on another culture; planning must be contextual, with solutions responsive to local conditions and mores.

cities and how their Chinese counterparts think through those issues. Such better understanding makes it possible to propose more practical and effective solutions to the subject." Tao was the first to pronounce that the Chinese participants had taught the Westerners a good deal in return.

At the most fundamental level, the way the Chinese treated one another during the workshop exemplified the code of any collaborative process. The ground rules were unspoken but uniformly obeyed: all team members' opinions must be given equal respect, and team members must not experience embarrassment in front of one another. Such courtesy would serve other workshops well.

The clarity of Chinese thinking, revealed in the students' ideas and articulate presentations, also inspired the Americans. The Chinese students were adept at explaining their work, justifying their course of action. Intense study accompanies all planning decisions in China, infusing civil service with an academic standard unusual in the United States. Even the politicians capably discussed planning and development issues.

The sojourn in China ratified the EDAW philosophy that a Western approach cannot be imposed wholesale on another culture; planning must be contextual, with solutions responsive to local condi-

tions and mores. The more layered the knowledge of a locale and its thinking, the more effective the endeavor. Marco Polo was a formidable advisor because he spoke the language, immersed himself in the culture, and spent two decades traversing the whole of China to hone his perception. It is plainly impossible to comprehend a society this profound in just a few weeks, making local participation indispensable to international consulting. EDAW/Pei demonstrated in Suzhou that a workshop infused with professional support from the host country is one effective way to structure such involvement.

As for the possible intrusion of a Western imperative, no one can thoroughly suspend perspective and training, nor can a consultant ignore a client's wishes. The city of Suzhou had solicited advice from outside precisely because Western expertise, for now, is a prized commodity in China. But it is the responsibility of the guest advisors to discern the extent of application, because not all foreign concepts fit. The ability to select techniques from abroad which are realistic and can be adopted in sympathetic fashion is a measure of the advisors' skill.

And what if local desires contradict Western wisdom? For example, the EDAW/Pei team presumed to save the "great and noble" Ping Jiang, historic preservation being an accepted part of city planning

Standing: Joe Brown and interpreter. *Seated:* Zhang Xinsheng,
mayor of Suzhou, C.F. Tao, developer and project sponsor, T'ing Pei,
and Qiu Xiaoxiang, Suzhou planning director.

The students unfurled a carefully drawn concept plan for Ping Jiang that synthesized the recommendations of all five teams. The plan is distinguished by a holistic approach that melds ideas from different disciplines, interweaving solutions to separate problems to advance a common goal.

as we know it. The Chinese agencies believed otherwise. In their estimation, the old quarter was outdated, in poor condition, and every bit as entitled to the benefits of modernization as prosperous cities in the West. The conflicting viewpoints were crystallized in the debate around introducing automobiles into the centuries-old pedestrian precinct. The Chinese demanded the car as basic to revitalization. But EDAW/Pei knew the consequences of traffic, air pollution, street widening, parking demand, and noise on the core of venerable cities. (Think of Athens and Rome.) Moreover, as global citizens, they felt responsible for protecting Suzhou, a resource so unique that it has been listed by UNESCO as a world heritage site. The outcome in the plan was the creation of vehicular loop roads that permit cars and trucks to enter the site but not to permeate it. Where a roadway must be widened, it echoes the original crooked alignment. The outcome in the minds of the Western landscape architects was a new appreciation for the dexterity and compromise that contextual planning can require.

In contrast to EDAW's experience with charrettes in American cities, where often too much is expected in a matter of days, the Chinese had no preconceived notion about what could be done. When the team produced a complex and practical plan that would clearly contribute to Suzhou, the client's satisfaction was very high. The amount of product alone—the thirty-two boards in ten days, illustrating landscape context, historic preservation, redevelopment and infrastructure—astounded the Chinese participants; it appeared the workshop had been under way for months. "Efficiency" was a unanimous word of praise from the students.

"We got more enthusiasm than we would ever have if it had been a three-month study," concluded Bob Pell, "and at the end of it we would have presented a plan, and everyone would have been very polite." Instead, there was a fascination with the process, an engagement in the decision-making, and real value placed on the final product.

The intelligence of the plan, the force of the collaboration, and the courage to make breakthroughs, were well rewarded with accolades and applause. But there was something bigger here, the inner satisfaction that comes from taking hold of the planning process. Shaping the city, shaping the future, is the alluring part of city planning which had apparently been denied to the Chinese students before. For this one time, their ideas and their colleagues' were unrestricted, intertwined, and fully realized; the students had seen the collective solution take form.

A swell of emotion is typical at the conclusion of EDAW's student programs. But the hugging and crying at Suzhou was not the ordinary drill; it suggested a rite of passage. "They wanted everything they could get from us. They had us autograph the sketches, the drawings, the brochures," Joe Brown said with a measure of triumph. Then, more pensively, "Hopefully, we can keep the plan alive."

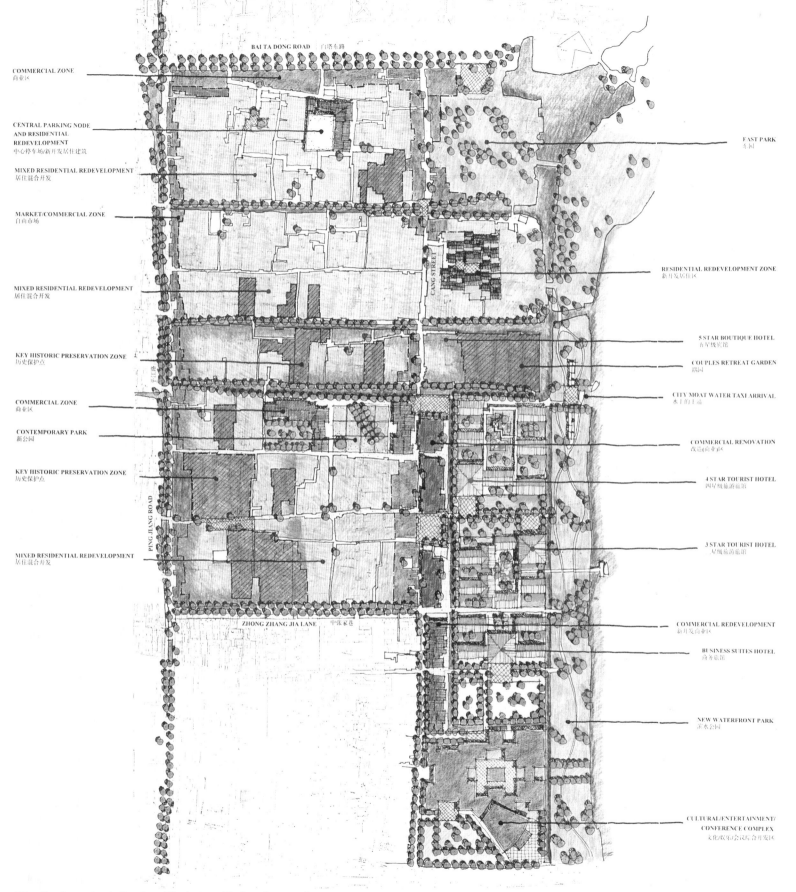

COMMERCIAL ZONE
商业区

CENTRAL PARKING NODE
AND RESIDENTIAL
REDEVELOPMENT
中心停车场/新开发居住建筑

MIXED RESIDENTIAL REDEVELOPMENT
居住混合开发

MARKET/COMMERCIAL ZONE
自由市场

MIXED RESIDENTIAL REDEVELOPMENT
居住混合开发

KEY HISTORIC PRESERVATION ZONE
历史保护点

COMMERCIAL ZONE
商业区

CONTEMPORARY PARK
新公园

KEY HISTORIC PRESERVATION ZONE
历史保护点

MIXED RESIDENTIAL REDEVELOPMENT
居住混合开发

BAI TA DONG ROAD 白塔东路

CANG STREET

PING JIANG ROAD

ZHONG ZHANG JIA LANE 中张家巷

EAST PARK
东园

RESIDENTIAL REDEVELOPMENT ZONE
新开发居住区

5 STAR BOUTIQUE HOTEL
五星级宾馆

COUPLES RETREAT GARDEN
耦园

CITY MOAT WATER TAXI ARRIVAL
水上的士品

COMMERCIAL RENOVATION
改造/商业区

4 STAR TOURIST HOTEL
四星级旅游旅馆

3 STAR TOURIST HOTEL
星级旅游旅馆

COMMERCIAL REDEVELOPMENT
新开发商业区

BUSINESS SUITES HOTEL
商务旅馆

NEW WATERFRONT PARK
滨水公园

CULTURAL/ENTERTAINMENT/
CONFERENCE COMPLEX
文化/娱乐/会议混合开发区

51

**The final product: Suzhou Workshop Redevelopment
Concept Plan for Ping Jiang.**

Epilogue

The period of east-west overland traffic did not last long; by 1405 the land passage to Cathay was closed to Europeans. "Marco Polo excelled all other known Christian travelers in his experience, in his product, and in his influence. The Franciscans went to Mongolia and back in less than three years, and stayed in their roles as missionary-diplomats. Marco Polo's journey lasted twenty-four years." —Daniel J. Boorstin, *The Discoverers*

Historically, China's receptivity to outside influence has been intermittent and short-lived. The opportunity to share Western experience in planning and preservation with our Chinese counterparts might be a fleeting one, and this imparted to the Suzhou workshop an unspoken urgency to communicate and accomplish as much as possible in a limited time. Will the process leave a modest trace, like the Franciscans, or a legacy like Marco Polo?

A visit to Ping Jiang within a year of the workshop would reveal little or no perceptible change. Yet in the months following July 1996, the benefit of the workshop could be measured in other ways. In pursuit of the plan, Mayor Zhang solicited hotel development and Planning Director Qiu negotiated with the silk factory to relocate, although he reported disappointedly that stipends to retired silk factory workers were affecting the cost, and therefore the viability, of a move. Qiu kept discussion alive with a recalcitrant provincial government to relocate the prison, and his staff began to design new, compatible housing for Ping Jiang. A crisp land use map entitled "Suzhou Metropolitan Area: 1996–2010" shows Ping Jiang entirely residential: no hotel complex, no commercial corridor, no special designation for the historic core, although it doesn't show the erstwhile prison or factories either. Qiu said that this is a function of the generalized scale of the map, and not a reflection on the city's commitment to the workshop vision.

EDAW published a handsome document to serve as ambassador for the workshop's recommendations. The path to official adoption of any city plan is long and steep in China, beginning with a municipal planning committee and ascending by way of the provincial government to consent in Beijing. While the good graces of the Suzhou government were liberally bestowed on the workshop, and the participation of prominent individuals is the best sanction the workshop plan could have, it does not appear that any procedure for formal adoption, even at the local level, has been initiated. As time goes by, the workshop plan must also compete for attention with the advice of other international experts who are courted by the Chinese.[21]

Essential is an on-site, proactive player with the time and authority to advocate not only for the plan, but for the central concept of master developer. Appointing a master developer is pivotal to achieving the cross-subsidy upon which improvements for local residents and historic preservation so thoroughly depend. The Westerners are relying on Vice-Governor Yang, Mayor Zhang, and Planning Director Qiu—the emissaries who attested to their commitment before I.M. Pei—and on the staff at the Suzhou Planning Bureau who took part in the EDAW/Pei process, to carry forward the important work done there. About the prospects for the plan, Qiu said, "This kind of workshop is just a beginning, and is academic, less or more. It's my dream maybe some day it will come true."

In a recent letter, C.F. Tao wrote from Hong Kong: "I am most concerned whether the revitalization of Ping Jiang will succeed. Certainly, I hope the EDAW/Pei workshop plan was of some assistance. It would be naive to expect that plan to be implemented in full. I am also experienced enough to know the revitalization will be a very long process (as it is for any historic city)."

There is no cause whatsoever for concern about the effect of the workshop on the students; it is precisely what C.F. Tao had desired. The students have gained the confidence and knowledge to help initiate preservation-sensitive development in locales throughout China, as these letters corroborate:

Architect Wang Ying wrote from Tsinghua University, the Harvard of China, to say that since Suzhou, she has been working on a "renewal program" for a historic district in Beijing similar in size to Ping Jiang. It is not an effort to increase tourism, she hastened to explain, having been the social conscience of the Suzhou workshop team, but a strategy to improve living conditions for the residents and protect historic buildings from damage. "Until participating in the workshop in Suzhou, I did not recognize that meeting growing demands for urban services and infrastructure were basic themes in historic city development. So I extended my attention to those aspects of the project, instead of overnarrow attention only on buildings. I try to do that in my working project now." She laments the scarcity of resources for shelter, services, and infrastructure, and for the preservation of traditional character in old Beijing.

A Suzhou native, Wang Yi writes from Tongji University in Shanghai that, thanks to EDAW/Pei, he comprehends "that a good urban design should not only be fantastic blueprints, but also practicable. The Suzhou workshop paid enough attention to the economic problems, such as the financial balance in the redevelopment, compared to other planning practices in China."

Lin Yun communicated in Chinese on an engineering 'calc sheet' from the Suzhou Industrial Township Design and Research Institute. He wrote in the simplified characters promulgated by the Communists, making it harder for older émigrés in California to translate. Lin Yun stressed his new respect for the characteristics of a specific city, wherever it may be. Development, he said in what amounts to a description of C.F. Tao's Suzhou Garden Villas, should be compatible with local traditions, but should have creative aspects as well that are appropriate for modern time: you don't want to copy history. The distinction he observed between the Suzhou workshop and Chinese city planning was the wide perspective and technical grounding that comes from professionals in different fields working closely together. He hoped that some day this approach would be universal.

Wu Jiang, a professor in architectural history at Tongji University, has won a preservation battle in Shanghai to prevent demolition of an unusual colonial house; built by a Chinese owner who worked for a foreign firm, it looks traditional on the outside, but inside has features quite Western for its time, and the Shanghai municipal government has agreed to recognize the merit of that. About the Suzhou redevelopment plan, Wu Jiang was proud: "It doesn't matter if the idea is useful or not. It give the people a new idea."

He Xiaojun, also at Tsinghua University, wrote to Liz Gourley in December from Beijing. "I guess San Francisco is warm now, but here is cold and dry. This winter there isn't snow. When I recall this summer in Suzhou, I feel very happy, to meet you, to know you. We had a very good time. We shared with the joy and also the difficulty."

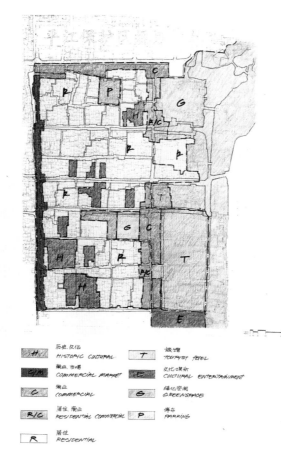

	历史 文化 HISTORIC CULTURAL		旅馆 TOURIST HOTEL
	商业 市场 COMMERCIAL MARKET		文化娱乐 CULTURAL ENTERTAINMENT
	商业 COMMERCIAL		绿化空间 GREENSPACE
	居住 商业 RESIDENTIAL COMMERCIAL		停车 PARKING
	居住 RESIDENTIAL		

Land use.

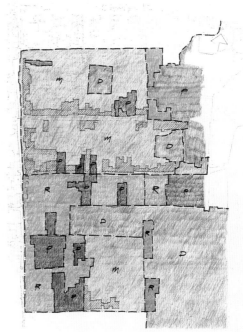

	保护 PRESERVATION
	改善 RENOVATION
	综合改造 MIXED DEVELOPMENT
	开发 DEVELOPMENT

Redevelopment zones.

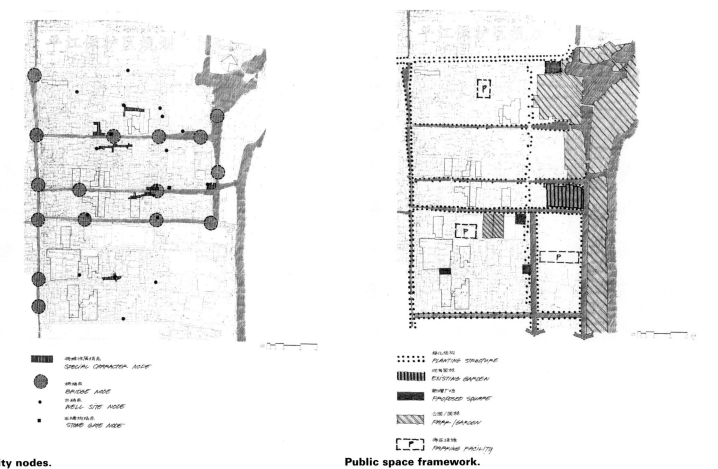

Activity nodes.

特殊性质结点
SPECIAL CHARACTER NODE

桥结点
BRIDGE NODE

井结点
WELL SITE NODE

石牌坊结点
STONE GATE NODE

Public space framework.

绿化结构
PLANTING STRUCTURE

纯角园林
EXISTING GARDEN

建议下场
PROPOSED SQUARE

公园/园林
PARK/GARDEN

停车设施
PARKING FACILITY

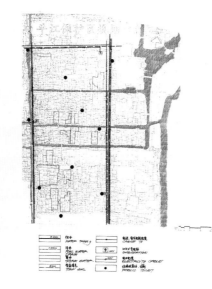

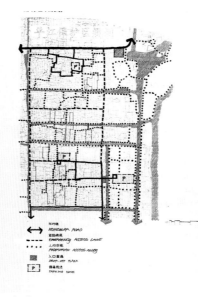

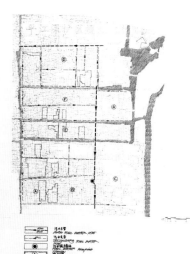

Infrastructure.

Circulation.

Drainage.

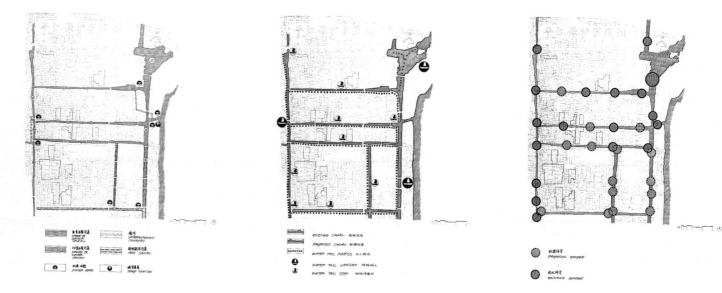

Canal improvements.

Canal framework.

Bridge framework.

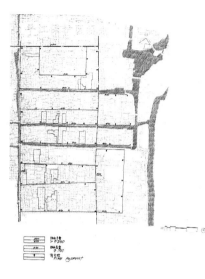

Water supply and fire hydrants.

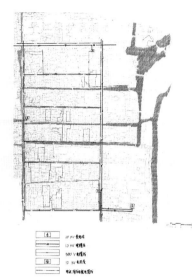

Electrical communications.

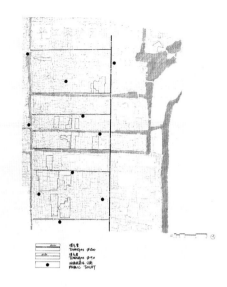

Gas lines and public restrooms.

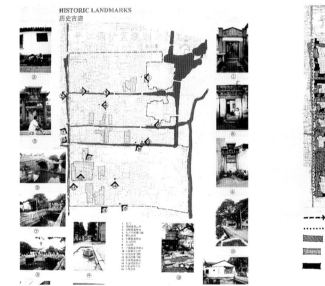

Historic landmarks.

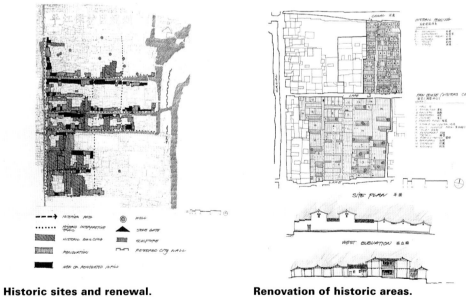

Historic sites and renewal.

Renovation of historic areas.

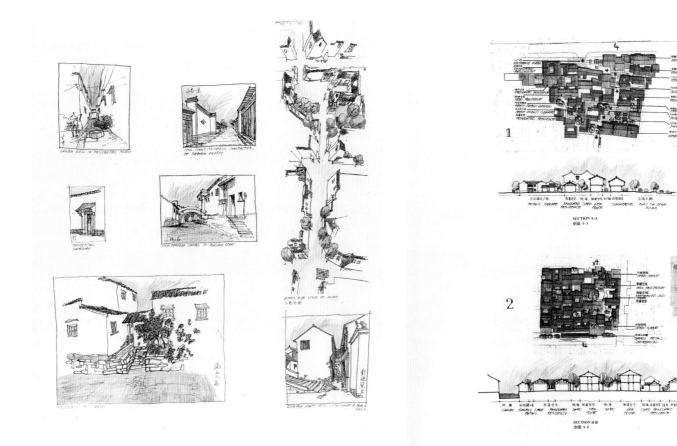

Historic character sketches.

Residential prototypes.

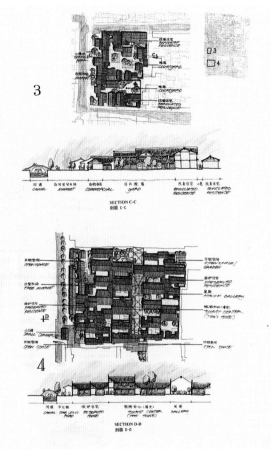

Residential prototypes.

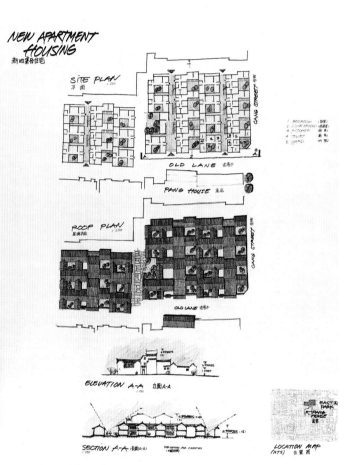

New apartment housing.

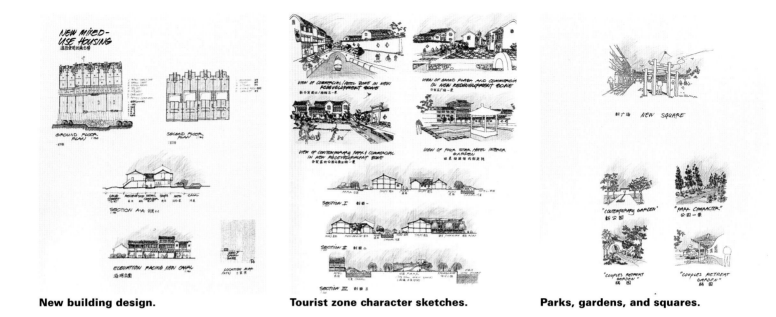

New building design.

Tourist zone character sketches.

Parks, gardens, and squares.

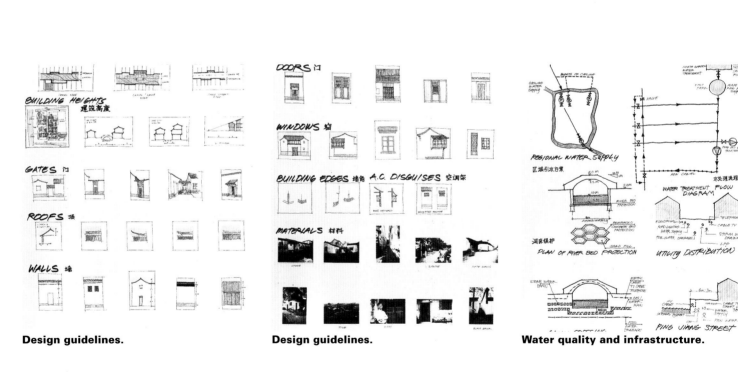

Design guidelines.

Design guidelines.

Water quality and infrastructure.

"CITY OF CANALS & BRIDGES" 小桥流水

WATER TAXI LANDING 水上的士站

BRIDGE STYLE 桥梁各种造型

EXISTING CONDITIONS ALONG DA XIN QIAO CANAL 大新桥地区现状

EXISTING CONDITIONS ALONG PING JIANG CANAL 平江河现状

PROPOSED REDEVELOPMENT OF DA XIN QIAN CANAL 改善后的大新桥地区

PROPOSED MARKET RELOCATION ALONG PING JIANG CANAL 改善后的平江河

Bridges and canals.

Bridges and canals.

SPECIAL NODE CHARACTER 景点

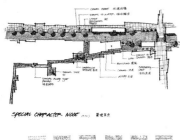

SPECIAL CHARACTER NODE 景德节点

PAVEMENT VARIATIONS 铺地

Streets, lanes, and alleys.

HISTORIC WELL SITE 古井

MARKET ALONG PING JIANG STREET 平江路市场

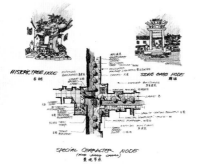

HISTORIC TREE NODE 古树

STONE GATE NODE 牌楼

SPECIAL CHARACTER NODE (PING JIANG CANAL) 景德节点

Streets, lanes, and alleys.

PEDESTRIAN ALLEY 步行道

PEDESTRIAN ALLEY 步行道

VEHICULAR ACCESS ROAD 车行道

EMERGENCY ACCESS LANE 消防车道

VEHICULAR ACCESS ROAD 车行道

Streets, lanes, and alleys.

Notes

1 Suzhou is known to many, including I.M. Pei, as "Soochow." In 1958, the People's Republic of China adopted the Pinyin system of romanization, and all spelling changed. Romanization is the approximation of Chinese pronunciation with letters of the Roman alphabet, without accounting for intonation, which also affects the sound of the word. As is modern practice, this book uses the Pinyin form, with the exception of words that have American usage, such as Yangtze for the river and T'ing for the younger Mr. Pei.

2 J.D. Brown in "Shang High," *Hemispheres*, February 1997, p. 70.

3 "The Yangtze valley alone has 300 million people, more than the entire U.S. That figure includes the hundreds of thousands of migrants who have flooded into the cities from rural areas looking for work." Ruth Eckdish Knack in "China Towns," *Planning*, August 1997, p. 15.

4 See plan, p. 9.

5 A hectare equals 2.47 acres, making the Ping Jiang study area roughly 100 acres.

6 For ease of narrative, the fourteen Chinese participants are referred to as "students," with the understanding that, even though a majority of them were professionally employed, they were at a formative stage in their careers and in attendance to learn from the workshop experience. The six enrolled at architecture school were in their early twenties; several of them were pursuing post-graduate studies. In addition, a working group of ten Chinese senior professionals was involved with the teams on a daily basis; eight were from Suzhou and commuted, while the two professors—Wu Jiang of Tongji University in Shanghai and Yang Jiangqiang of Southeast University in Nanjing—resided at the hotel. Ten resource bureaucrats addressed the gathering the first week and were available on call. Add the two workshop sponsors, three international observers, and eight western designers, and, all told, the workshop marshaled 47 people.

7 Driven by the cruel determination of Sui Dynasty Emperor Yang Di, some 5.5 million men excavated the entire Grand Canal in only six years' time. "By 1980, silt, poorly planned dams, water gates and irrigation systems, or plain atrophy, had reduced internal waterways mileage in China to a third of that in the 1960s." *China*, Lonely Planet travel guide. The Grand Canal is now 1100 miles long.

8 Greater Suzhou consists of three levels: the center city, the six county-level cities, and one hundred−odd satellite villages, for a total population of 5.7 million in 1994.

9 Dong Wu is the ancient kingdom name of Suzhou. The king of Wu, who founded Suzhou in the sixth century B.C., is reputedly buried on Tiger Hill.

10 In *Leisurely Sentiments Jotted Down*, quoted in *Chinese Classical Gardens of Suzhou*.

11 "Centralized air conditioners produced by the foreign-funded Suzhou Aim Far Air Conditioner International Co. Ltd. have been chosen by the renovation project of the Great Hall of the People in Beijing. . . ." Perhaps Suzhou Aim Far could be of some assistance in Ping Jiang. Reported by Han Guojian, "Suzhou: An Ancient City With A Modern Outlook," at http://china-window.com.

12 The subject of Pell's dissertation was the impact of the Long March on Chinese foreign policy in Africa in the 1960s.

13 Reference to the Clarke Quay ideal for Suzhou.

14 Land is not purchased outright in China; the government owns all the land, and releases it for a fixed time period, the length of time depending on the use. There are two types of ownership: national *(guoyou)*, owned by the central government, and mass *(jiti)*, owned by the peasants, the commune, or the township.

15 "Chinese officials can also demand money under regulations that no outsider can see posted anywhere. So the Singaporeans polled companies to discover what fees they were being charged, compiled a catalogue that listed hundreds of them, and submitted it to Suzhou authorities. After long discussions about the need for a pro-business environment, the voluminous list was pared to a mere 28." *Fortune*, "Global Report on Singapore and Suzhou," March 4, 1996, p. 183.

16 As observed by Pierre Clément and Sophie Charpentier-Clément in *Mimar*, June 1988, plazas in the European sense, defined by the facades of surrounding buildings, are not a characteristic feature of Suzhou. "Soochow and Venice, Two Cities on Canals," pp. 10-16.

17 Vehicular access will be a minimum of 7 meters wide, emergency access will be a minimum of 4 meters wide, thus reducing standard dimensions but accomodating necessary service in a safe manner.

18 I.M. Pei does not profess to be a sculptor; presumably the group envisioned an architectonic piece, like Pei's 1989 bell tower at the Shinji Shumeikai sanctuary, located near Kyoto, Japan.

19 The widening of scenic lanes to accommodate water and sewer lines—and the demolition of urban fabric which ensues—is a serious problem in other Yangtze River cities, such as Yangzhou, Changzhou, and Changshu. *Planning*, op. cit.

20 The principles of *feng shui*, the Chinese system of arranging space to attain a favorable destiny, were never discussed.

21 Since 1991, French architects (affiliated with the new town of Cergy-Pontoise, northwest of Paris) have been involved, revising their Master Plan for Suzhou in 1994. In 1997, two young planners from France took up residence to work on another district in the old city, and students at the Harvard Graduate School of Design examined Tiger Hill and environs, under the sponsorship of C.F. Tao.

Additional Sources

Boyd, Andrew. *Chinese Architecture and Town Planning: 1500 B.C.–A.D. 1911*. Alec Tiranti, London: 1962.

Cannell, Michael. *I.M. Pei: Mandarin of Modernism*. Carol Southern Books, New York: 1995.

Cummings, Joe and Robert Storey. *China–A Travel Survival Kit*. Lonely Planet, Third Edition. Berkeley, California: 1991.

Hockney, David and Philip Haas. "A Day on the Grand Canal with the Emperor of China, or Surface Is Illusion But So Is Depth." Milestone Film & Video, New York: 1991.

Hong, Liang. "From Harvard to Suzhou: Mayor Zhang Xinsheng Links East With West." *China Information*, May 1996.

Liu Dun-zhen. Translated by Chen Lixian and edited by Joseph C. Wang. *Chinese Classical Gardens of Suzhou*. McGraw-Hill, Inc. New York: 1993.

Pearson, Clifford A. "Updating a Chinese Tradition: Canal-Side Living." *Architectural Record* Pacific Rim Section, July 1996.

Tanzer, Andrew. "Stepping Stones to a New China?" *Forbes*, January 27, 1997.

Walsh, James. "The TIME Global 100." *Time*, December 5, 1994.

Participants

**EDAW/PEI
International Workshop**

Suzhou, China

T'ing Pei
Chairman/CEO, Pei Group (Holdings) Ltd.

Joseph E. Brown
President/CEO, EDAW

Bob Pell
Managing Director, EDAW PLC

Patrick Lau
EDAW earthasia

James Stickley
EDAW San Francisco

Elizabeth Gourley
EDAW San Francisco

Jeff Rapson
EDAW Denver

Leung Chen Wan
Scott, Wilson, Kirkpatrick
Hong Kong

Sponsors
Yan Daoming
Director
Suzhou Urban Construction Bureau

C.F. Tao
Chairman
New Heritage Development Ltd.

Students
Zhuang Yu, M. Arch, Ph.D. Candidate
Department of Architecture
Tongji University, Shanghai

Wang Yi, B. Arch, Postgraduate Student
Department of Architecture
Tongji University, Shanghai

Wang Ying, B. Arch, Postgraduate Student
School of Architecture
Tsinghua University, Beijing

He Xioajun, B. Arch, Postgraduate Student
School of Architecture
Tsinghua University, Beijing

Wan Chengxin, B. Arch, Postgraduate Student
Department of Architecture
Southeast University, Nanjing

Qi Gang, B. Urb, Urban Planner
Suzhou City Planning Bureau

Yao Helin, B. Urb, Urban Planner
Suzhou City Planning Bureau

Li Feng, B. Urb, Urban Planner
Suzhou Urban Planning Institute

Zhang Qin, B. Arch, Architect
Suzhou Construction Committee

Tan Donglin, B. Urb, Urban Planner
Suzhou Construction Committee

Lin Yun, B. Arch, Architect
Suzhou Industrial Park
Architectural Design Institute

Zhu Tao, M. Arch, Architect
Suzhou Architecture Design & Research Institute

Lu Zhen, B. Urb, Urban Planner
Suzhou Urban Planning Institute

Ye Jing, Undergraduate Student
Department of Architecture
Southeast University, Nanjing

Suzhou Working Group
Qiu Xiaoxiang, MUP, Arch
Managing Director
Suzhou City Planning Bureau

Shi Kuang, Senior Architect
Chief Planner
Suzhou Industrial Park Administration Committee

Wu Jiang, Associate Professor
Department of Architecture
Tongji University, Shanghai

Li Feng, Senior Engineer
Engineer-in-Chief
Suzhou City Planning Bureau

Tan Yin, Architect
Assistant Director
Suzhou Construction Committee

Shao Jianlin, M. Eng
Engineer
Suzhou Construction Committee

Yang Jiangqiang, Associate Professor
Department of Architecture
Southeast University, Nanjing

Zhou Guankang, Senior Urban Planner
Suzhou City Planning Bureau

Chen Xikun, Engineer
Suzhou City Planning Bureau

Gu Rende, Senior Landscape Architect
Engineer-in-Chief
Suzhou Urban Planning Institute

Interviewees
Qiu Xiaoxiang, MUP, Architect
Director
Suzhou City Planning Bureau

Lu Siukun
Deputy Director
Suzhou Planning Committee

Wei Zhonghuan
Deputy Director
Suzhou Economic Committee

Zhang Fenghang
Deputy Director
Suzhou Land Administration Bureau

Xu Minsu
Deputy Director
Suzhou Tourism Bureau

Han Xian Yun
Deputy Director
Suzhou Land Administration Bureau

Zhang Huanrong
Engineer-in-Chief
Suzhou Public Utilities Bureau

Zhan Yongwei
Engineer-in-Chief
Suzhou Garden Administration Bureau

Wang Renyu
Vice Director
Suzhou Office of Relics Protection and
Administration

Zhou Renyan
Governor
Ping Jiang District

Afterword

The question of preserving China's ancient and historical cities in the face of the unprecedented and explosive modernization and industrialization of the country is one of the most important issues to be tackled entering the new millennium. This was the challenge I asked my son T'ing to address on behalf of our family's native city of Suzhou.

Together with his colleagues from the firm of EDAW, Inc., they have prepared a set of guiding principles for one of the most sensitive districts of Suzhou which can show the way for the redevelopment and revitalization of the area while maintaining and enhancing its historical character. This is a formula which can surely be adapted to other ancient cities in China and perhaps elsewhere.

As with any plan, however, the ultimate question is whether there is the political will and administrative capacity to see it through to execution. This does not mean that it has to be pursued inflexibly, as conditions are constantly in flux, but it does mean that there should be a long-term determination to go from a plan to implementation. This is an excellent plan, and I sincerely hope that the responsible authorities will do their utmost to bring about its realization.

—I.M. PEI